OECD Territorial Reviews

Competitive Cities

A NEW ENTREPRENEURIAL PARADIGM
IN SPATIAL DEVELOPMENT

ORGANISATION FOR ECONOMIC CO-OPERATION AND DEVELOPMENT

ORGANISATION FOR ECONOMIC CO-OPERATION AND DEVELOPMENT

The OECD is a unique forum where the governments of 30 democracies work together to address the economic, social and environmental challenges of globalisation. The OECD is also at the forefront of efforts to understand and to help governments respond to new developments and concerns, such as corporate governance, the information economy and the challenges of an ageing population. The Organisation provides a setting where governments can compare policy experiences, seek answers to common problems, identify good practice and work to co-ordinate domestic and international policies.

The OECD member countries are: Australia, Austria, Belgium, Canada, the Czech Republic, Denmark, Finland, France, Germany, Greece, Hungary, Iceland, Ireland, Italy, Japan, Korea, Luxembourg, Mexico, the Netherlands, New Zealand, Norway, Poland, Portugal, the Slovak Republic, Spain, Sweden, Switzerland, Turkey, the United Kingdom and the United States. The Commission of the European Communities takes part in the work of the OECD.

OECD Publishing disseminates widely the results of the Organisation's statistics gathering and research on economic, social and environmental issues, as well as the conventions, guidelines and standards agreed by its members.

This work is published on the responsibility of the Secretary-General of the OECD. The opinions expressed and arguments employed herein do not necessarily reflect the official views of the Organisation or of the governments of its member countries.

Also available in French under the title:
Examens territoriaux de l'OCDE
Villes et compétitivité
UN NOUVEAU PARADIGME ENTREPRENEURIAL

© OECD 2007

No reproduction, copy, transmission or translation of this publication may be made without written permission. Applications should be sent to OECD Publishing rights@oecd.org or by fax 33 1 45 24 99 30. Permission to photocopy a portion of this work should be addressed to the Centre français d'exploitation du droit de copie (CFC), 20, rue des Grands-Augustins, 75006 Paris, France, fax 33 1 46 34 67 19, contact@cfcopies.com or (for US only) to Copyright Clearance Center (CCC), 222 Rosewood Drive Danvers, MA 01923, USA, fax 1 978 646 8600, info@copyright.com.

Foreword

Spatial development has always been a primary policy objective in urban policy because in a physical space where population and activities are densely concentrated, provision of basic functionalities of space, such as shelter, mobility and sanitation, have been an important prerequisite for public welfare. In fact, during the period of massive urban expansion, urban policy meant, above all, policies to cope with rapidly expanding public demands for urban space and services.

Since economic globalisation and the subsequent intensification of inter-city competition placed urban economic competitiveness on the top ladder of urban policy agenda, increasing attention has been paid to the profound change in the governance of cities and urban regions, particularly in the field of urban spatial development.

The change is often described as a shift from a managerial mode of governance, which is primarily concerned with effective provision of social welfare services to citizens, to that of entrepreneurialism, strongly characterised by a pro-economic growth strategic approach, risk-taking, innovation and an orientation toward the private-sector.

This shift opened up a new policy dimension in urban spatial development, created numerous policy innovations, and produced spectacular results in successful cases. However, policy experience over the past decades has shown that challenges exist for policy planners to realise the full potential of entrepreneurial approach in urban spatial development and prepare their cities for the flourishing knowledge economies in the 21st century.

To exchange and share the policy experience in urban policy among the member countries, the Territorial Development Policy Committee (TDPC) and its Working Party in Urban Areas (WPUA) have, since its creation in 1999, been providing a unique forum for policy dialogue, through which this study has also been produced.

FOREWORD

> **Acknowledgements.** *This report was directed by Eiji Torisu, Head of the OECD Division of Regional Policies for Sustainable Development, and drafted by Eiji Torisu (Chapters 1, 2 and 5), Tetsuya Shimomura (Chapter 3) and Patrick Dubarle (Chapter 4).*
>
> *Chapter 2 of the report draws on the outcomes of "the OECD International Symposium on City Attractiveness", which was held in 2005 in Nagoya city, Japan. The OECD would like to thank Ministry of Land, Infrastructure and Transport of Japan, Aichi Prefecture, City of Nagoya, Urban Renaissance Agency, Chubu Economic Federation, and Nagoya Chamber of Commerce and Industry for co-hosting the symposium. The OECD would also like to thank all the speakers who participated in the symposium for making important contributions to produce this report.*

Table of Contents

Executive Summary.	7
Chapter 1. Introduction: The Entrepreneurial Approach in Spatial Development	15
1. Spatial development in an urban and regional context	16
2. Competitiveness agenda and spatial development.	17
3. From managerialism to entrepreneurialism	18
4. Characteristics of urban entrepreneurialism	19
5. Fragmentation.	24
6. Emerging issues and the entrepreneurial approach	26
7. Structure of this book.	27
Chapter 2. Urban Entrepreneurialism and Policies to Make Cities Attractive	29
Introduction	30
1. An overview of past and current measures to enhance city attractiveness	31
2. Key issues: overcoming urban policy dilemmas	45
Conclusions: pitfalls in the entrepreneurial approach.	60
Chapter 3. A Market-oriented Approach in Building and Housing Policies .	65
Introduction	66
1. Policy reviews	66
Conclusion.	94
Notes	95
Chapter 4. Spatial Planning for Competitiveness	97
Introduction	98
1. The development of urban planning in several major cities: evidence of the changing role of spatial planning.	99
2. Strategic planning policies and frameworks	104
3. Collaborative planning and network-based urban governance. . . .	107
Conclusions: challenges and future perspectives	117
Notes	119
Chapter 5. Conclusion.	121
1. Pitfalls of "narrowness"	122
Bibliography	127

Boxes

1.1.	Market-led planning.	21
1.2.	Strategic planning.	23
1.3.	Urban regime theory	25
2.1.	Strategic plan to revitalise Bilbao.	36
2.2.	The Baltimore Model	38
2.3.	Cultural clusters	43
2.4.	Budget diversion: Birmingham's case	58
2.5.	The Northern Way	61
3.1.	Point system for evaluating development proposals, Fort Collins, United States.	72
3.2.	Performance-based planning system, Australia	73
3.3.	Outline of the housing information package in France	79
3.4.	Outline of the Home Information Pack, United Kingdom.	80
3.5.	Registration system of Rental Housing Available for the Elderly (RHAE) and Rental Housing Exclusively for the Elderly (RHEE), Japan.	83
3.6.	"Client's choice" programme, Woonbron-Maasoevers, the Netherlands	93
4.1.	Co-ordination across jurisdictions.	111
4.2.	The *Plan Local d'Urbanisme* in France (PLU) and the *Schéma de Cohérence Territorial* (SCOT)	113
4.3.	The different levels of planning	115

Tables

3.1.	Development of performance-based building codes in OECD countries.	68
3.2.	Size of the resale market compared to owner-occupied housing in selected OECD countries	76
3.3.	Proportion of owner-occupied housing, per income distribution quartile and household type, 1982-1998 (in %).	86
3.4.	Development of distribution of households in social housing, 1980s-1990s	91
3.5.	Housing stock development goals (Delftwonen, the Netherlands).	92
4.1.	Trends in spatial planning	101

Figures

3.1.	Requirements for developing the housing resale market in Japan.	75
3.2.	Number of Right to Buy sales, England, 1980-2001	85
3.3.	Trends of tenure in England	87
3.4.	Representation of income groups in social rented housing.	88
3.5.	Form of housing tenure in the Netherlands by income decile, 1981-2002.	89

ISBN 978-92-64-02240-9
OECD Territorial Review
Competitive Cities
A New Entrepreneurial Paradigm in Spatial Develompent
© OECD 2007

Executive Summary

Competitiveness agenda has profoundly changed the mode of urban governance...

Economic globalisation and the subsequent intensification of inter-city competition have caused a profound change in the governance of cities. It is the change in the mode of policy planning from managerialism, which is primarily concerned with effective provision of social welfare services to citizens, to entrepreneurialism, which is strongly characterised by pro-economic-growth strategic approaches, risk-taking, innovation and an orientation toward the private-sector.

The change has been most evident in urban spatial development, which has long been preoccupied with the managerial mode of policy making, ultimately aiming at efficiently managing the diverse spatial needs by land-use control and infrastructure provision. Fundamental changes began to emerge in the 1970s, initially in the policies for inner city problems, which had then become increasingly evident in many large cities, particularly previously affluent industrial cities. The policy response to these problems had long been "additional public service provision to people with special needs".

However, as the root cause of the problems has gradually begun to be diagnosed as the collapse of the economic infrastructure there, the policy approach started to change drastically, from targeting more and more public resources into such areas to meet "special" or "additional" needs, to creating new industry and new jobs by attracting an economically active population back into the inner areas and regenerating the economic infrastructures.

The entrepreneurialism has also been a dominant approach in former industrial cities that were struggling to restructure their economic base. However, it has further spread into more buoyant cities with growing industries, and even into the most successful world cities, such as New York, London and Tokyo, becoming the mainstream of urban policy planning. Such shift has been accelerated by the dynamism in urban hierarchy created by economic globalisation, and by an edgy insecurity at all levels of the urban hierarchy where today's success is not guaranteed to continue tomorrow.

With the irreversible trend of global economic integration, there is a growing recognition among policy planners that the only way that cities can secure competitive advantages over their perceived competitors in an ever-intensifying inter-city competition is by pursuing entrepreneurial strategies. Under such circumstances, entrepreneurialism is becoming a key feature in urban policy, and it is now widely acknowledged that the extent to which a city can achieve this paradigm shift will determine its competitiveness in the global market.

Entrepreneurial approaches have distinctive characteristics...

The new approaches in urban spatial development, commonly referred to as "urban entrepreneurialism", have some distinctive characteristics. First, it ultimately aims at fostering and encouraging local economic development. Hence, it is intrinsically initiatory and pro-economic growth, trying to initiate economic growth rather than control and manage it. In the context of spatial development policy, it takes the form of "positive planning", which tries to create economic growth by pro-active means, as compared to the traditional "passive planning", which is more concerned with the management of land-use.

Second, while the previous approaches were basically led by the public sector, the new approaches are becoming increasingly market-driven, aiming at making full use of market mechanisms to achieve public goals with less public intervention.

Third, urban entrepreneurialism involves fundamental change in the attitudes towards, and relationship with, the private sector, being both pro-private-sector and willing to collaborate with it. Strategic alliances were formed between the public and private sectors, and public-private partnership provides the essential institutional framework for cities to compete in the global market by combining private resources and expertise with local governmental powers.

Lastly, policy planning in the new approaches shows strong characteristics once distinctive to private businesses, such as risk-taking, inventiveness, promotional and profit motivation. Many methods employed by policy planners originated in the private sector. Above all, strategic planning forms the backbone of the new approaches, as a means to plan effectively for and manage the future at a time when the future itself appears increasingly uncertain.

Entrepreneurial approaches have produced diverse policy innovations in urban spatial developments...

This shift towards urban entrepreneurialism opened up a new dimension in urban spatial development by bringing in various policy innovations, which have been achieved by applying corporate strategic planning methodology to public policy planning. Resources have been strategically allocated for spatial development to maximize the positive effects of city promotion and branding. In fact, policy measures for urban economic regeneration have been increasingly centred around image-enhancing and place-marketing initiatives to project cities as attractive place to live, work and invest. Measures called "imagineering" and "re-branding" have been extensively employed to redefine and re-image cities endowed with negative images inherited from the industrial era. Flagship developments have been employed as "hard-branding" to produces a significant impact on city image with their large scale, high profile, and innovative design by internationally-famed architects.

The entrepreneurial approaches identified and exploited new potential for urban economic regeneration in such policies as cultural policy and event-hosting, which do not traditionally belong to the urban policy portfolio. Whereas cultural policy used to be pursued essentially as a welfare service to provide access to artistic and cultural heritages for wider social groups, it has now acquired a status as a strategic tool for city promotion, based on the premise that it possesses the potential to enhance city image and attractiveness as well as to boost urban tourism. It is also expected to contribute to the diversification of the local economic base by encouraging local cultural production to grow into major knowledge industries.

In the policies for building and housing, which form the physical fabrics of urban space, entrepreneurial approaches aim to harness the private sectors' power for urban spatial development, and exploit market potential to the fullest by introducing new modes of regulatory measures to stimulate private innovation and strengthen market functioning.

Fragmentation in various forms...

The rapid mainstreaming of urban entrepreneurialism caused significant changes in urban spatial development policy over the past years. The changes are characterised by fragmentation in one form or another.

From government to governance

Fragmentation occurred in the institutional framework for spatial development, taking the form of change from government towards governance. New kinds of partnerships have been formed between actors within formal governments, and between formal governments and the economy and civil society; increasingly spatial development policy is formed by a wide range of organisations and their partnerships, rather than local governments acting as the single and foremost agent to plan and implement spatial development strategies as has traditionally been the case.

The real power to form spatial development strategies lies within a broader coalition of forces within which government and administration have only a facilitative and co-ordinating role to play. In this framework, policy planning is no longer a process of hierarchical government but a complex process that involves coalition formation and negotiation. This diffuse and multi-faceted form of rule through diverse actors has become a predominant characteristic of the institutional framework that supports urban entrepreneurialism in spatial development.

Project-based approaches

Emphasis on the encouragement of private investment created the tendency for urban planning to be fragmented into individual projects, with comprehensive city planning giving way to project-driven practices. Partnerships and coalitions were also formed on a specific project basis. Such practices often resulted in a piecemeal approach to urban development that lacked strategic foresight or long-term planning, posing a difficulty for citizens to see where their cities are going.

Fragmented planning ideologies

Varied degrees of emphasis on the importance of competitiveness objectives between cities, levels of governments, policy planners and citizens created fragmentation in the form of sharply different policy agenda among actors in spatial development, as in cases where strong pressure by the central government is in sharp contrast with local governments that still see their role in terms of traditional public service provider.

Policy pitfalls must be avoided...

Urban entrepreneurialism has produced spectacular results in successful cases, demonstrating its potential for urban economic regeneration. However, in other cases, it was revealed that urban entrepreneurialism was hardly adequate in addressing the long-standing urban issues that it was conceived for in the first place. In worst cases, it has been criticised as having widened the various forms of division in cities. Such mixed results appear to indicate that urban entrepreneurialism is not a panacea, and policy experiences over the past decades have shown that challenges exist for urban entrepreneurialism to realise its full potential and prepare itself for the new policy context in the 21st century by overcoming certain pitfalls.

Building unique assets

First, too much dependence of planners on a handful of successful cases as "good practices" resulted in an ironic situation that place-marketing, which originally aimed at differentiating a city from others, has in fact seriously undermined the local distinctiveness and uniqueness of many cities, and created "analogous cities", which refers to the situation where it is difficult to differentiate a city from others both in actual physical forms and place marketing narratives. Planners' efforts to appeal to stereotyped images of knowledge workers' tastes also contributed to the creation of built-environments that are strongly characterised by similarities in tastes and their consumption-oriented nature, which favours selected social groups with considerable disposable income.

Similarities have not only been evident in physical renovation policy but also in promotional incentives offered to external investors. The adoption of similar templates for city promotion strategies by cities that engage in place competition would trigger the competition of "offering more of the same", which in turn would create a buyers' market and undermine the efficacy of such strategies that entail considerable financial burdens on tax-payers.

Urban entrepreneurialism has aimed at being creative in policy planning; however, the emergence of analogous cities and analogous strategies appears to cast doubt on strategies that attempt to pursue strategies similar to those already employed more successfully in other locations, and clearly point to the necessity to re-construct future policy planning around the notion of identifying and building up unique local assets rather than focusing too much on image creation. Place promotion without unique local assets would fail to leave long-lasting effects on the local economy.

Avoiding short-termism

Past policy experience strongly indicates that in order for urban entrepreneurialism to address effectively long-standing urban issues, it is necessary to incorporate policy measures to translate short-term impacts gained by city promotional strategies into long-term effects on local economies. Such a process requires local capacity to assimilate short term economic gains into long-standing economic restructuring. Thus, policy efforts to build up local economic capacity are essential, and these are precisely what have often been neglected by policy planners who are under pressure to maximise short-term gains by attracting external elements.

Short-termism arising from profit-maximising motives in entrepreneurial approaches creates the danger of precluding longer-term perspectives for city competitiveness. In fact, many local governments are allocating increasingly high budgets to city promotion strategies as manifestation of their entrepreneurialism. However, excessive occupation with the narrow aspects of city promotional objectives sometimes obscures the importance of long-term efforts towards local capacity-building. When the fiscal constraints on local capacity-building programmes, such as education, job-training and technological development of local firms, are aggravated by loss-making flagship developments, which have been promoted as profit-making at the outset, the detrimental effects on the local economy would be considerable. The highly volatile nature of property markets would further heighten the risks involved. Policy planners should reflect soberly on what is at stake in adopting such high risk strategies and where the balance should lie.

The neglect of long-term policy could lead to the dualism of image and reality, where city promotion strategy simply becomes a "carnival mask" that creates the impression of regeneration and vibrancy within cities, but, in reality, does nothing to address the underlying problems that necessitated regeneration programmes in the first place. Such a situation is what urban policy planners should avoid.

Holistic approach

Urban policy planners are increasingly required to address wider policy objectives; not only economic but also social, environmental and cultural policies are demanding policy planners' attention. It is also expected to play a positive role in a global policy agenda rather than simply reacting to it. This sea change will have implications for urban entrepreneurialism.

What has become clear from past experience is that optimality in certain policy objectives does not necessarily correspond to optimality in others. Thus, strategies based on narrowly defined policy objectives would not result in the improvement of overall outcomes, with broader social, cultural and environmental objectives often residualised or diluted as they tend to be overridden by a centralised agenda of economic objectives.

Hence, urban entrepreneurialism should adopt more holistic approaches by incorporating wider policy objectives into coherent and complementary strategies. For example, market-led approaches, which have become the guiding principle due to their capacity to respond to rapid changes, should aim at achieving wider policy goals by positively interacting with market forces, not simply by following them.

Learning process through wider participation

Public-private partnership provided a collaborative framework that is flexible and efficient. However, the narrowness of the scope of stakeholders that participate in the process has often made it difficult for residents to share the strategies coming out of such partnerships. The corporatist mode of decision making sometimes created the image that important decisions were made behind closed doors in an elitist circle to which ordinary citizens did not have proper access. The absence of effective means of securing accountability has been criticised as "the private management of public policy", and further made it difficult for citizens to share the entrepreneurial philosophy exercised in such processes. Such criticism suggests that urban entrepreneurialism has often failed to secure citizen support, which is crucial for the long-term viability and effectiveness, as well as the democratic legitimacy, of entrepreneurial strategies.

An entrepreneurial urban economy will only emerge through an active process to nurture entrepreneurial culture among residents. All the actors in the local economy, including residents, business executives and government officials, have to learn how to be entrepreneurial. However, thinking and behaving entrepreneurially, or competitively, is not something that actors know how to do automatically. To engender widespread entrepreneurialism among residents, residents' capacity for strategic thinking should be enhanced by an inclusive policy process. They should be allowed a chance to think strategically about the economic issues that policy planners face. To build such capacity in residents, learning is essential, and an inclusive and open process in strategy planning with a wide range of participants would offer such an opportunity.

Learning to collaborate in such a "communicative and collaborative planning" process would develop a richer and more broadly-based understanding, through which collective approaches to resolving conflicts may emerge. Securing wider participation in the strategy planning process should provide such learning experience. Future urban entrepreneurialism should be supported by an institutional framework that represents such accountability, empowerment and partnership.

New role of local governments

The widened scope of participants will pose a challenge for local governments. There is a widespread concern about the efficacy of traditional local government structures and practices in planning in the face of the shift from government towards governance. To continue to play a central role, they need to develop new styles of operation which are amenable to contemporary modes of governance. This would require a departure from hierarchical and bureaucratically-determined practices that are driven by rules and regulations and which are slow to respond to new demands that arise.

New modes of entrepreneurial urban governance would be increasingly structured by organisational forms involving negotiative networks stretching across governments, governmental agencies, private and third-sectors, and there would be significant change in the mode and culture of interaction between them. In order to prepare for that change, local governments will need to operate in a more pluralist way than in the past, alongside a wide variety of public and private actors. It will be their task to stimulate and assist other actors to play their part instead of, as well as, making provision themselves. In other words, the emphasis in the role of local governments would shift towards "enabling governments" from "providing governments". This creates a new emphasis on negotiation and network-building skills in the public sector.

These capacities would enable local government planners to mobilise effective networks which could work in an integrated fashion towards achieving broad environmental, economic, social and cultural planning aims. By strengthening such capacities, local governments would continue to play the central role in the process of policy making and implementation as mediators and catalysts, with their unique strategic overview, local expertise and sensitivity to local interests. A strong and coherent leadership role played by local governments is crucial for urban entrepreneurialism to flourish in the fragmented structure of urban governance.

Final question...

The essence of urban entrepreneurialism is to apply innovative thinking to policy planning in a strategic way, based on long-term vision. Such attitude is an essential property not only of competitive private enterprises in the global market, but also of competitive cities in inter-city competition on a global scale. Urban entrepreneurialism should manifest itself in identifying and building up unique local assets, in harnessing "old policy tools" with totally new perspectives, and in mobilising the collective potential of all the actors in the local economy by motivating and empowering them.

The question that a policy planner employing an entrepreneurial approach should always ask himself is just how entrepreneurial his approach is in this sense.

ISBN 978-92-64-02240-9
OECD Territorial Review
Competitive Cities
A New Entrepreneurial Paradigm in Spatial Develompent
© OECD 2007

Chapter 1

Introduction: The Entrepreneurial Approach in Spatial Development

This chapter provides an overview of how economic globalisation has caused a profound change in the mode of policy planning in urban spatial development. It reviews how entrepreneurialism, a new paradigm for urban spatial development, differs from the traditional approach of managerialism, which has been primarily concerned with the management of urban land use and the provision of public services and infrastructure. Finally, it analyses the three forms of fragmentation that the entrepreneurial approaches have created in the policy framework for urban spatial development.

1. INTRODUCTION: THE ENTREPRENEURIAL APPROACH IN SPATIAL DEVELOPMENT

Over the past decades, increasing attention has been paid to the profound change in the governance of cities and urban regions, particularly in the field of urban spatial development, which was triggered by economic globalisation and the subsequent intensification of inter-city competition. It is often described as a change from a managerial mode of governance, which is primarily concerned with effective provision of social welfare services to citizens, to that of entrepreneurialism, strongly characterised by a pro-economic growth strategic approach, risk taking, innovation and an orientation toward the private-sector. This chapter gives a brief overview of how such a profound change in policy planning took place in urban spatial development when the competitiveness agenda emerged on the central stage of urban policies.

1. Spatial development in an urban and regional context

Spatial development has always been a primary policy objective in urban policy because in a physical space where population and activities are densely concentrated, provision of basic functionalities of space, such as shelter, mobility and sanitation have been an important prerequisite for public welfare. In fact, during the period of massive migration of population into large metropolitan areas, urban policy meant, above all, policy measures to cope with rapidly expanding demands for urban space and co-ordinate conflicting spatial needs. Together with infrastructure provision to strengthen the functionality of urban space, the primary policy tools have been spatial planning and development control, which jointly aim at controlling and managing urban land use.

The excessive concentration of population and economic activities in a small number of metropolitan areas was regarded as a problem that required policy measures on a national scale because of its sheer magnitude. Many OECD countries introduced policy measures at the national level in the form of national development plans, new city developments outside metropolitan areas, inter-regional transport infrastructure, relocation programmes on a national scale consisting of development control in metropolitan areas and relocation incentives for rural areas.

The re-allocation of population and economic activities from congested metropolitan areas was also supported by regional policy which considered widening regional disparities in terms of a problem of national coherence, not simply in terms of significant negative externalities in urban areas. Hence, regional policy makers thought it also necessary to achieve a more balanced national structure by re-allocation measures. At this stage, the convergence occurred between the policy objectives of urban and regional policies. Furthermore, apart from the difference in the geographical scope of policy planning, policy approaches in spatial development both in urban and regional policies shared similar characteristics, in that both approaches were fundamentally "managerial", that is, the ultimate objective was to manage the land use of people and the economy by land use regulation and infrastructure provision.

2. Competitiveness agenda and spatial development

Fundamental changes in urban policy making initially occurred in the previously affluent industrial cities of developed countries where so-called "rust-belt" industries were concentrated when the economic globalisation plunged these cities into an unprecedented scale of economic decline. For example, during the 1970s, the industrial base of Birmingham in the United Kingdom shrank by a third, and manufacturing employment in Sheffield contracted from 139 000 in 1971 to 58 000 in 1987. The rapid rate of decline of former industrial cities presented a stark contrast to the increasingly buoyant economies of other cities strongly characterised by service sector industries and other new types of economic activity.

An example that illustrates this change best is inner city problems, which became increasingly evident in many large cities in the advanced economies since the 1970s. Inner city problems have long been considered as essentially a residual problem of the welfare state (Deakin and Edwards, 1993). More precisely, the problem was identified as the concentration of people with special needs. Consequently, the policy response was to target more resources into the deprived areas to provide for the additional and special needs to be found there; in other words, it was basically service provision to those people. For example, the Urban Programme and the later Community Development Projects in the United Kingdom were primarily concerned with "additional" service provision to those people in "areas of special social need" where living conditions are particularly poor with poverty, high levels of unemployment, poor housing and inadequate community services (Home Office, 1974). This was a traditional "welfarist" response to what was perceived as a concentration of need. It was resource allocation according to need by targeting the areas where poverty concentrated rather than by selecting targets on the basis of a means test.

However, once the diagnosis of the fundamental problem transformed to the view that the root cause of the coincidence of physical decay and social deprivation in the inner cities was the collapse of the economic infrastructure there, the policy approach began to change drastically. The economic activity upon which the residents of these areas had depended so long for their livelihood had simply disappeared; either it had migrated elsewhere or it had died in situ. The problem was compounded by socially selective population-loss from the inner cities, leaving behind very high dependency ratios and the decline of the economic infrastructure in the areas.

The change in the perception of the aetiology of the problem indicated that the idea that inner city problems could be solved or even alleviated by targeting public resources into such areas to meet "special" or "additional" needs had became defunct (Deakin and Edwards, 1993). It was recognised that additional provision of public services for the "residue of the unfortunate that the welfare state had not yet reached was a misconceived, palliative and probably futile" strategy. What needed to be done was clear: new industry, new jobs, and an economically active population had to be attracted back into inner city areas in order to regenerate the economic infrastructure.

However, it was also a diagnosis that posed formidable challenges for urban policy planners, who have traditionally been adopting managerial approaches, because it was painfully evident that old policy tools, more or less characterised as problem-solving and distributional, were hopelessly inadequate for the new policy objectives. It demanded a totally different mode of policy planning: one which was innovative and strategic, willing to explore all kinds of avenues through which to alleviate distressed conditions and thereby secure a better future for their populations. In other words, an "enterprise culture solution" (Deakin and Edwards, 1993). Such a recognition fundamentally altered policy approaches; they would be significantly different from those prior to the 1970s, which were usually both initiated and implemented by the public sector, whose objectives reflected a strong inclination towards the social dimension.

The inner city problem is a prime example of a change in the perception of a problem drastically re-aligning policy approaches. Since then, the view that economic competitiveness forms the basis of the population's standard of living and welfare has gradually permeated into other policy fields, fundamentally altering their policy planning; urban spatial development was no exception.

3. From managerialism to entrepreneurialism

The reorientation in urban policy planning from public service provision to private enterprise promotion caused a profound change in policy approach, which has been described as a change "from managerialism to entrepreneurialism" (Harvey, 1989). The adoption of such a totally different attitude has been accelerated by the growing recognition among urban policy planners that the only way that cities can compete in an increasingly unpredictable and globalised economy is by pursuing pro-active strategies designed to secure competitive advantages over their perceived competitors.

Such an attitude in urban policy planning is commonly referred to as urban entrepreneurialism. It envisages positive and strategic measures based on a pro-active approach, rather than a problem-solving one, together with new institutional structures of urban governance. Over the past years, the managerial approach has steadily given way to the entrepreneurial approach. Although this shift from managerialism to entrepreneurialism has not been straightforward, and both approaches usually co-exist, with the pace of transition very much dependent on local economic and social conditions, the entrepreneurial approach has further spread into the more buoyant cities with growing industries, and even into the most successful world cities, such as New York, London and Tokyo, becoming the mainstream of urban policy planning. Thus, the shift from managerialism to entrepreneurialism defined a broad context in urban policy planning over the past decades.

Behind the ubiquity of the entrepreneurial urban approach is the dynamism in urban hierarchy created by the internationalisation of economic activities, the increased geographical mobility of production and investment, and "an edgy insecurity at all levels of the urban hierarchy" (Hall and Hubbard, 1998) where today's success is not guaranteed to continue tomorrow. Under such circumstances, a general consensus has developed recently among urban policy planners that positive benefits are to be gained by cities taking an entrepreneurial stance towards economic development.

The appearance of many cities adopting this new approach has been described as the emergence of "entrepreneurial cities" (Hall and Hubbard, 1998). It invokes images of cities as analogous to firms, whereby the self-interested actions of cities competing for economic growth are supposed to generate benefits for all urban residents and, ultimately, for all the cities involved in the competition (Leitner and Sheppard, 1998). It was thought that if key local economic and political actors could just get their acts together and if urban management focused on economic regeneration rather than on the "welfare" issues that had unfortunately preoccupied policy makers in the past, a new era of urban economic development would emerge (Lovering, 1995).

4. Characteristics of urban entrepreneurialism

In urban spatial development, entrepreneurialism has primarily been directed towards exploiting economic development opportunities dormant in local areas in need of urban regeneration. Therefore, although it took various forms in different policy contexts, it demonstrates some shared characteristics consistently.

4.1. Pro-economic growth approach

The new approach aims to foster and encourage local economic development as its main objective. Hence, it is intrinsically initiatory and pro-economic growth, trying to create and initiate economic growth rather than control and manage it. Re-orientation also took place in spatial development policy, which explicitly took on the role of initiator of economic growth. It took the form of "positive planning" as compared to "passive planning", which is a traditional approach to spatial development more concerned with the management of demand for urban land use rather than initiating it. Such a shift was inevitable because while traditional spatial planning takes for granted the private sector's interest in using urban land; in areas with scarce interest by private firms to invest there was little left to plan for. Therefore, the traditional approach to spatial development had almost been rendered powerless. It was necessary to have a totally new pro-economic growth style of policy planning in spatial development.

4.2. Market-led approach

Second, new approaches are fundamentally market-driven, whereas formerly they were led by the public sector. This was most clearly manifested in the United States, where many waterfront redevelopments were instigated by private-sector initiatives, but in other developed countries market principles have also been explicitly encouraged.

With the maturity of the market economy, the market has become the main field and tool for policy planners to implement policies and achieve their goals. Although there is no single, unequivocal definition of the market-oriented approach, a key concept is to make full use of market mechanisms, rather than public intervention, to achieve public goals, such as the provision of public goods, the improvement of public services, and solving economic and social problems. Within this general orientation, it can take various forms. For example, Brindley, *et al.* (1996) identify three types of market-led planning approaches (see Box 1.1).

It is said that the market-led approach is gradually changing the nature of the role that governments (central and local) perform. They have long been preoccupied with the direct provision of public infrastructure, urban services and urban land use control, but are increasingly taking on the role of enabler and facilitator, rather than that of regulator and provider.

Box 1.1. **Market-led planning**

Trend planning

Trend planning aims at enhancing market functions based on the recognition that the regulative style of spatial planning is ineffectual in addressing urban problems. Originally, the term was used to illustrate the situation where planners have little choice but to follow market forces. However, later it acquired a more positive meaning as a planning approach that reorientates spatial planning towards a private-sector perspective. It envisages the planning system reflecting market trends in the allocation of resources, and planners are charged with facilitating development in line with market demand. It aims to streamline the planning system and reduce delays, and explicitly introduces market criteria into development control decisions. The priority is private-sector development activity and responsiveness to market forces by helping private investors and developers to co-ordinate and manage their investment plans.

One example of this approach is the Simplified Planning Zone (SPZ) in the United Kingdom. In a SPZ, a scheme of permitted uses will be prepared for each zone and any conforming development will not require planning permission.

Leverage planning

Leverage planning puts emphasis on the potential of the private sector to solve the problem, and uses public-sector finance to stimulate a weak market and to release a greater volume of private-sector investment by effectively subsidising, either directly or indirectly, private-sector developments that might not otherwise have gone ahead. It also adopts a flexible attitude to development proposals. For example, the designation of Enterprise Zones in the United Kingdom brought exemption from certain taxes, development land taxes and industrial training levies, both for existing land-users and businesses and for those wishing to move in. Incentives include tax allowances, direct and indirect subsidies, infrastructure provision, and land reclamation by the public sector to reduce land acquisition costs for private developments.

The prime example of leverage planning is the policies pursued by the London Docklands Development Corporation (LDDC) in the 1980s. It was overtly manifested that its primary objective is to generate private-sector investment.

Leverage planning aims to regenerate a market in land and property development through public-sector subsidies, infrastructure and site preparation. It also uses profits generated by rising land values for further pump-priming. Therefore, its applicability depends on the degree of private-sector interest in the areas. Such situation is illustrated by the mixed results brought about by the various Urban Development Corporations (UDCs) in the United Kingdom.

> ### Box 1.1. **Market-led planning** (cont.)
>
> **Private management planning**
>
> Private management planning is based on the recognition that the recovery of the most deprived and rundown areas of our towns and cities should be achieved not by massive state intervention, but by handing over the management of the whole renewal process to the private sector. It aims at bringing in not only private-sector financial resources but also the managerial methods, skills and experience of the private sector, trying to harness its dynamism, creativity and energy with the co-operation of local people and business.
>
> In the United Kingdom a new type of private sector, managed and funded city development agencies, was proposed in the early 1980s to bring deprived inner areas up to national standards in housing and employment. Council estates were also disposed to private developers for renovation and resale to allow them to take over such areas. In a few cases the process has been extended to private-sector involvement in the actual management of renewal, through the mechanism of a non-profit private trust. Under this strategy, private-sector agencies take on tasks that were previously seen as the exclusive responsibility of the public sector. Stockbridge Village, Knowsley, in the United Kingdom is a key example. The former GLC estate at Thamesmead has also been taken over by a trust.
>
> Source: Brindley, T., Y. Rydin and G. Stoker (1996), *Remaking Planning: The Politics of Urban Change*, Routledge, London.

4.3. Public-private partnership

As literature on public entrepreneurship defines it as "the process of creating value for citizens by bringing together unique combinations of public and/or private resources to exploit social opportunities" (Morris and Jones, 1999), urban entrepreneurialism involves the fundamental change in the attitudes towards, and relationship with, the private sector economy, being fundamentally pro-private-sector and showing a strong willingness to collaborate with it. The public-private partnership has become the predominant institutional framework within which to plan and implement regeneration strategies. This change was driven by the recognition that, in the face of intensifying global competition between cities for mobile factors of economic growth, a coalition between public and private sectors provides a strategic basis for competition. Partnership and entrepreneurialism are the guiding principles in this coalition.

Public-private partnership created an institutional framework where traditional local boosterism is combined with the use of local governmental powers to try and attract external sources of funding, new direct investment, or new employment sources. Through this mechanism, private sectors were increasingly involved in the planning process, and it was often the case that the private sector took the initiative. This tendency is particularly evident in the United States, where civic boosterism and entrepreneurialism had long been a major feature of urban policy. It was observed that the reduction in the flow of federal redistributions and local tax revenues after 1972 led to a revival of boosterism, and state and local governments were characterised as "the last entrepreneurs" (Goodman, 1979).

4.4. Strategic approach

The strengthened relationship with the private sector also changed policy thinking, and the new approach shows strong characteristics once distinctive to businesses: risk-taking, inventiveness, promotion and profit motivation. Many methods employed by this approach, such as strategic planning and place marketing, also originated in the private sector. Above all, strategic planning, originally developed by large corporations to plan effectively for and manage their futures at a time when the future appeared increasingly uncertain, formed the backbone of the new approach to spatial development, and became a policy tool that was widely used by urban practitioners in the 1980s.

Although a great deal of variation can be found in the usage of strategic planning, there are some common features, such as: 1) clarification of overall objectives; 2) setting short-term, achievable goals; and 3) involvement of a wide range of stakeholders (see Box 1.2).

Box 1.2. **Strategic planning**

Albrechts (2001) summarises strategic spatial planning for the public sector as a process that:

- Is directed at a limited number of key strategic issues, scans critically the environment, in terms of determining strengths and weaknesses in the context of opportunities and threats, scans the external trends, forces and the resources available.
- Identifies and gathers major stakeholders (public and private).
- Allows for a broad and diverse involvement during the planning process.
- Develops a (realistic) long-term vision/perspective and strategies taking into account the power structures, uncertainties, competing values; designs plan-making structures and develops content images and decision frameworks through which to influence and to manage spatial change.
- Is about building new ideas – and about building processes that can carry them forwards – generating ways of understanding, ways of building agreement, ways of organising and of mobilising to influence in different arenas.
- Is oriented towards decisions, actions, results and implementation in the short- as well as in the medium- and long-term, and incorporates monitoring, feedback and revision.

5. Fragmentation

The new approach was gradually adopted in various aspects of spatial development, such as spatial planning, urban renovation and housing, drastically changing the policy orthodoxy well-established for decades. Alternative measures have been rigorously sought after, and much policy innovation took place during the course of policy restructuring. Such a process has inevitably created various repercussions in policy framework. Above all, fragmentation is the most conspicuous and significant. The past decades have seen the systemic fragmentation of the established approaches (Healey, 2006). Established procedures were perceived as breaking down, in different ways, in different areas of governance activity.

5.1. From government to governance

Firstly, fragmentation occurred in the institutional framework of spatial development. Established institutions, particularly local governments, were considered obsolete and posing impediments to private investment by being unable to catch up with the reality of the globalised economy. In such cases, they were abolished and/or special agencies were set up with mandates by central governments to override the powers traditionally exercised by local governments.

Privatisation, deregulation and multi-actor policy making are key ingredients of the new policy making, which reflect the shifting balance between government and society: away from the public sector and more towards the private sector. New kinds of "partnership" have been formed between actors within formal governments and between formal governments, the economy and civil society; and it is increasingly becoming the case that urban policy is formed by a wide range of organisations and their partnerships rather than local governments acting as the single and foremost agent to plan and implement urban policies, as they have traditionally been. This fundamental change in the form of institutional framework for urban policy planning is often described as a "change from government towards governance".

The real power to reorganise urban life often lies elsewhere, or at least within a broader coalition of forces within which urban government and administration have only a facilitative and co-ordinating role to play (Harvey, 1989). Urban policy planning is no longer, if it ever was, a process of hierarchical government, but rather a complex process that involves negotiation, coalition formation, indirect influence, multi-institution work and public-private partnership. This diffuse and multi-faceted form of rule has come to be termed "governance" (Painter, 1998). The urban regime theory is a theory that describes such change in urban policy planning (see Box 1.3).

> **Box 1.3. Urban regime theory**
>
> Urban regime theory was developed in the United States as an interpretation of urban politics that took seriously both the informal aspects of politics and the reliance of local state and local politicians on non-governmental resources in achieving political objectives.
>
> For example, Stone (1989) argued that the governance of Atlanta, Georgia since the Second World War could only be understood if due weight was given to the role of key individual and institutional actors outside the formal structures of city government and particularly to the informal relationships developed between such actors and the politicians. What makes governance in Atlanta effective is not the formal machinery of government, but rather the informal partnership between city hall and the downtown business elite. This informal partnership and the way it operates constitute the city's regime; it is the means through which major policy decisions are made.
>
> Source: Painter, J. (1998), "Entrepreneurs Are Made, Not Born: Learning and Urban Regimes in the Production of Entrepreneurial Cities", in T. Hall and P. Hubbard (eds.), *The Entrepreneurial City: Geographies of Politics of Regime and Representation*, Wiley, Chichester.

Instead of nesting neatly in a hierarchical model of levels of government responsibility, new urban governance is characterised by "heterachy", which might be defined as "rule through diversity" (Painter, 1998), involving actors from a variety of different levels of government, a wide range of private and semi-private bodies, from the level of the European Union to local neighbourhood organisations (Healey, 2006). Since this re-alignment of governing and control can be observed on all scales and hierarchy levels, new forms of neighbourhood governance, as well as global governance, have developed (Keil, 2006).

5.2. Project-based approaches

Secondly, emphasis on the encouragement of private investment brought about the situation where urban planning fragmented into individual projects. Systematic "comprehensive" town planning is giving way to a project-driven practice which seeks to encourage private investment by targeted incentives. Deregulation is also introduced on an individual project basis in the form of special planning zones that permit deregulation of a specific locality. Enterprise Zones in the United Kingdom, Urban Renaissance Zones in Japan, and many other similar schemes introduced in the OECD countries are such examples, sharing similar features such as de-regulation of planning controls, tax rebates and other incentives to promote private investment projects in designated statutory zones.

Partnerships and coalitions were formed on a specific project basis, and the ephemeral nature of many coalitions tends to result in a piecemeal approach to urban development that lacks strategic foresight or long-term planning, which sometimes made it difficult for citizens to see where their cities were going. On the other hand, there have also been numerous examples of local alliances and partnerships characterised by relative longevity. Such coalitions appear to be based on a clear understanding of the objectives of the coalitions, strong leadership capacity and (often) the presence of a visionary individual prepared to act as the figurehead for the regime (Hall and Hubbard, 1998).

5.3. Fragmented planning

Finally, the emergence of the competitiveness agenda in urban policy planning created a situation where policy priorities vary considerably according to the economic, social and political conditions specific to the individual locality. Brindley, et al. (1989) argue that such a transitional moment in planning history when one dominant ideology of planning attempts to replace another created the fragmentation of planning, and identified six different styles of planning thus created. The fragmentation of planning often represented the widening disparity in the policy agenda among different players in the policy planning process. For example, it has often been observed that the strong emphasis by central governments on the economic competitiveness agenda was in stark contrast to the policy priorities of local governments who still see their role very much in terms of traditional public service provider.

6. Emerging issues and the entrepreneurial approach

After economic competitiveness appeared on the mainstream agenda of urban policy, priorities and policy making in spatial development significantly changed over the past decades. The new approach brought about remarkable success in a number of cases that opened a new dimension in urban spatial development by proving that spatial development could positively initiate economic development and raise living standards. However, in other cases, as will be examined in the following chapters, it was revealed that urban entrepreneurialism was hardly adequate in addressing persistent urban issues. In worst cases, it has been criticised as having widened the various forms of division in cities. The successful cases demonstrated that urban entrepreneurialism does have potential that the traditional approach does not have; however the mixed results indicated that entrepreneurialism is not a panacea that can be applied in a uniform fashion no matter what local conditions are. Then, what are the preconditions for entrepreneurial approaches towards spatial development to effectively address the long-standing urban issues for which urban entrepreneurialism was originally conceived?

Furthermore, recent concerns over the durability of the model of our society are introducing new policy objectives in every policy agenda, and sustainable development is becoming a binding concept in new policy approaches. Urban policy is no exception. Urban space, because of its dense concentration of population and economic activities, has significant implications on sustainability on a national or even a global scale. Urban policy planners have long been concerned with the long-term durability of cities in economic, social and environmental terms, and this concern is extending beyond the interests of individual cities.

As the well-known phrase "think globally, act locally" illustrates, regional and urban policies are increasingly expected to play a positive role in a global policy context rather than simply reacting to it. Does this change in the urban policy agenda, which reflects the sea change in national and global policy discussion, necessitate further change in the policy approach to spatial development which has already been carried out, that is, the revolutionary development from a "managerial to entrepreneurial" mode? If the answer is "yes", how should it change? These are the questions being asked to urban policy planners today.

7. Structure of this book

This book looks into these questions by taking examples from some major topics in urban spatial development policy: urban regeneration, housing, building and spatial planning. Each case, after reviewing how new policy approaches have been developed by incorporating urban entrepreneurialism, explores how the above questions are being posed in each policy context and what changes are emerging. In the final chapter, efforts will be made to identify the challenges that urban policy planners have to overcome in order to bring entrepreneurial approaches into full fruition, and indicate the broad directions in which OECD countries are heading.

ISBN 978-92-64-02240-9
OECD Territorial Review
Competitive Cities
A New Entrepreneurial Paradigm in Spatial Develompent
© OECD 2007

Chapter 2

Urban Entrepreneurialism and Policies to Make Cities Attractive

Chapter 2 reviews how urban entrepreneurialism manifests itself in the policies for urban regeneration, which have been increasingly focusing on presenting a city as an attractive place to live, work and invest in for knowledge workers. It looks into three major groups of urban regeneration strategies: city branding, flagship developments and culture-led and event-driven strategies. It identifies pitfalls that policy planners should avoid in order to obtain long-lasting benefits from entrepreneurial approaches for urban economic regeneration.

Introduction

The prime example of urban entrepreneurialism could be found in the urban policies that have been increasingly adopted by many cities since the late 1970s, particularly by old industrial cities that have experienced an unprecedented magnitude of industrial decline. In such a situation, it was natural that policy planners looked to external investors and entrepreneurs to revitalise their local economies. By doing so, the necessity for cities to present positive images of themselves to the outside world captured the attention of policy planners, who recognised that image assumes ever greater importance in the post-industrial economy. While the entrepreneurial transformation of place identity is thus seen as an essential means by which cities can attract business, enhancing their position in the inter-urban competition, it has also been argued that it plays an internal role in galvanising local support and fostering civic pride, potentially gathering widespread support for entrepreneurial policies. Changing the image of a city was, thus, becoming a central component of entrepreneurial governance.

It has come to be widely recognised that one of the most obvious manifestations of entrepreneurialism among city governments has been the attention devoted to the transformation, or at least enhancement, of the image of the city (Hall and Hubbard, 1998). Consequently, programmes for urban economic regeneration have been driven more and more by image-enhancing initiatives, to such an extent that urban spatial development is increasingly becoming constituted around the narratives of entrepreneurialism envisioned by, among other things, place promotion. Thus, city marketing is the principal driving force in urban economic regeneration. The logic that more jobs make a city better is giving way to the realisation that making a city better attracts more jobs (Bailey, 1989).

The new approach has necessitated a fundamental re-alignment of policy agenda around city promotional goals based on strategic planning to strengthen city attractiveness and competitiveness and promote growth creation in the new global economic climate. The central idea is to present the city as an attractive place to visit, live, work and invest in the global market where mobile capital and knowledge workers find their destinations. Therefore, these promotional measures adopted by cities for economic regeneration can be viewed as efforts to enhance city attractiveness.

Spectacular results have been achieved in successful cases. However, past experience also suggests that there still remain important issues that need to be addressed urgently in order for the potential of urban entrepreneurialism to be fully exploited. The objectives of this chapter are: first, to review the profound changes in the mode of policy planning that were caused by urban entrepreneurialism in urban spatial development focusing on policies to make cities attractive; second, to evaluate the achievements by identifying both their valuable contributions to policy planning and their shortcomings in addressing urban issues.

1. An overview of past and current measures to enhance city attractiveness

The application of urban entrepreneurialism to spatial development has produced significant policy innovation. Policy strategies have been considerably diversified by incorporating various tools whose potential has recently been recognised. New staples of these policies, which include flagship property developments in city centres with spectacular architectural designs, establishing new cultural facilities, hosting major cultural and sports events, festivals and fairs and city branding, were originally conceived for different purposes, but are now being extensively used for urban regeneration objectives as measures to present a city as an attractive place to live and work. At the core of these diverse policy tools is strategic planning to put the various policy components in a coherent context, and city branding, which plays a crucial role in producing the identity that a city wants to convey.

This section will discuss the specific policies that have become essential components of urban economic regeneration strategies: city branding, flagship city centre developments, culture-led policies and event-driven policies.

1.1. City promotion and city branding

Almost every city now has a series of promotional pamphlets, posters and other cultural products communicating selective images of the city as an attractive, hospitable and vibrant international city in which to live and work (Barke and Harrop, 1994). In fact, city promotion has a long history as one of the basic tools to attract people and money, such as visitors, immigrants, firms and new investment, to cities for economic development purposes. However, the recent surge of interest in city promotion, particularly in city branding, may be ascribed to the widely shared recognition that reconstruction of a city's image is the starting point of urban economic regeneration, since many cities are realising that their images as industrial cities are excluding them from the cognitive map of knowledge workers in their location decisions.

In place marketing, a city as an entity is often likened to a "product" that supplies a labour market, land and premises to businesses, and housing, urban services, security and places to socialise to residents, as well as the basic utilities of infrastructure. The reason for conceptualising a city as a product is to apply the established methodology for commercial product marketing, of which the most important aspect is branding, to city promotion.

A brand is defined as "a multidimensional assortment of functional, emotional, relational and strategic elements that collectively generate a unique set of associations in the public mind" (Aaker, 1996). This unique set of associations forms a "brand image" of the product, which differentiates it from other similar products by summing up what it connotes or means in the eyes of the public (Patterson, 1999). Hence, brand images help consumers to identify a product by simplifying diverse attributes that the product possesses.

Place branding tries to apply the same methodology employed in commercial product marketing to geographical locations, and is understood as "an attempt to create and nurture the narratives that give meaning to a place" (Julier, 2005) and differentiates it from many others in location choices by highlighting its core benefits, style and culture (Bennett and Savani, 2003). The rise of interest in place branding for marketing purposes can be partly explained by the fact that many cities can be easily substituted for other cities in location decisions because of the increasing mobility of people and capital and the decreasing importance of location constraints imposed by transport costs, which had decisive impacts in the previous industrial era.

Place marketing does not only promote the existing virtues of a city, but seeks to redefine and re-image a city by altering negative images. This conscious manipulation and promotion of new imagery of cities has been termed "imagineering" by the pioneers of the Disney theme parks. Similarly, when place branding is used to fundamentally alter the prevailing perception of a place and establish a completely new brand image, it is called re-branding. "Imagineering" and "re-branding" have been extensively employed by major post-industrial cities whose place images are deeply associated with decline, dereliction, pollution, deprivation and labour militancy inherited from the former industrial era. These images, which are often reinforced by occasional media portrayals of crime and public disorder in those cities, tend to be perpetuated, and city imagineering and re-branding are expected to dispel such negative images and replace them with new and positive ones.

1.1.1. Limitations of city branding

On the other hand, the limitations of applying branding methodology for commercial products to place branding to form a new place-identity have come to be known. One example is the "issue of multiple identities", which refers to a situation where a brand image suitable for one group of stakeholders may be inappropriate for others (Bennett and Savani, 2003). The attributes a city or a region possesses are basically not a single product but an agglomeration of identities and activities that are not conducive to a simple summing-up as is customary in the branding process of commercial products. If planners try to unreasonably simplify such a complex entity into a brand image that targets corporate investors and upper-class urban professionals, the citizens may feel that it does not correctly reflect or promote their reality, and it may fail to secure their support. In fact, considerable criticism has been directed to manipulation of city image through re-branding and imagineering whereby city identities are "sanitised, commodified and distorted in accordance with the perceived demands of the global marketplace" (Hall and Hubbard, 1998).

Experience shows that place branding works best when the values of a brand are rooted in the aspirations of the people. Hence, the brand images to be employed in a place re-branding process should reflect the local distinctiveness, characteristics and identities. City promoters wishing to quickly discard the existing negative images often try to create brand images that look appealing to entrepreneurs, investors and the creative workforce but are not necessarily rooted in the existing local attributes. Diverse local ethnicities and a range of social class groups also make it difficult to develop brand images that appeal to the aspirations of a wide range of stakeholders. It is also said that the inconsistent attitudes of local politicians make it difficult for clear brand images to develop.

Therefore, the challenge for policy planners is to coalesce the multiple identities of various stakeholders into a concise and easily-understood brand that appeals to the types of people and businesses they want to attract without compromising indigenous cultures, local distinctiveness and identities. Achieving this requires an institutional framework whereby various stakeholders are brought together to discuss and develop a shared version of new brand images. However, an investigation of 22 urban regeneration units in some major cities (Bennett and Savani, 2003) revealed that this type of framework is not being established. In most cases, key decisions concerning brand identity were "handed down" to the regeneration units, which were then charged with the task of implementing them. Many units conducted formal and routine consultation procedures with representatives of trade, business or employer associations, but few possessed formal and regular procedures for consulting representatives of resident groups. In addition, the investigation found that the period of time for making decisions concerning re-branding was far too short compared to the amount of time necessary to build relationships with local residents and businesses.

The issue of multiple identities often led to "one brand, many messages" practices among local governments, by which they transmitted different messages to different stakeholders, such as businesses, property-owners, and pre-existing and potential residents (Bennett and Savani, 2003). This approach was in part a reaction to a fear that a uniform projection of certain messages would antagonise particular interest groups. For example, messages implying rising living costs, property prices and rents were not included in materials intended for existing residents. Such practices made it extremely difficult to apply integrated marketing communication, which ensures that audiences perceive a consistent set of messages.

1.1.2. Effectiveness of place branding

A more fundamental question is the effectiveness of the current practice of place branding as a method of place marketing. First, branding images often appear bland and undifferentiated to the external audience. For example, a survey on language employed in place branding among city authorities around the world revealed a substantial degree of homogeneity in their use of terms. They frequently describe their cities as dynamic, cosmopolitan, diverse, vibrant, and cultural (Julier, 2005). It is essential for "a strong sense of identity to emerge from the words and pictures if a promotional publication is to make an impact" on audiences (Burgess, 1981). However, because virtually every city tries to project a similar set of brand images in promotional publications, audiences can spot little difference between them. This would explain the weak impact of city promotion activities on their target audience.

Second, there is the problem that information disseminated by city promotion can be assimilated by the audience only in an extremely selective way. This is because individuals tend to be more receptive to information that conforms to the beliefs and thinking they already possess, while they tend to ignore information that contradicts those beliefs (Gold, 1980). In this regard, regional stereotypes, or "negative images", play a particularly important role, since branding images that fail to conform to regional stereotypes are normally treated either as untrue or as an unimportant exception to the general rule (Gold, 1980). For example, a survey that sought to measure the effectiveness of promotional advertising by the northern centres and areas in Britain revealed remarkably low awareness of it among managers (Business Decision Ltd., 1974). Resistance to promotional information that is not in accordance with regional stereotypes widely held by the public makes it very difficult to alter them.

Although it would be possible to develop clear, easy-to-understand narratives of a city by applying the same branding methods used for commercial products and communicating them to the expected audience through various media, they would sound hollow if they failed to reflect the reality and the material circumstances of the city. This is precisely the reason why it is becoming important to distinguish between the processes of selling and marketing in the practice of marketing. Selling is a process whereby advertising is determined by the product being sold. Marketing, however, is a process whereby advertising determines, or at least shapes, the product for sale: what one has to sell is shaped by some idea of what the consumer wants. The same would apply to the case of cities. The distinction between "selling the city" and "marketing the city" is becoming crucial for policy planners who are engaged in place promotion.

However, the adoption of place branding in city promotion creates the risk that it will be perceived merely as a tactical sales operation whereby convenient imagery is attached to messages directed towards various constituencies, rather than an important strategic framework to organise all the urban regeneration efforts based on the new brand. The latter could be called a strategic approach, while the former could be called an operational approach. Past experience clearly shows that place branding should be conceived as a strategic approach, where a new brand is positioned as a guiding framework around which broad urban regeneration programmes are organised to establish new brand images as a reality. Place marketing, thus, should be much more than merely selling an area to attract mobile companies or tourists. It should be viewed as a fundamental method of guiding the development of places in a desired fashion (Fretter, 1993), and the formation of place-identity through place branding should be regarded as a process of creating the reality to be promoted through city marketing. Physical renovation, such as flagship city centre developments, which will be examined in the following section, was conceived to bring city branding images to reality by giving material form to them.

1.2. Physical renovation and flagship developments

Physical environment provides the tangible basis of city attractiveness. It not only provides the basic functionality of a city but also gives it character. Superb physical environment is in itself an important element in attractiveness, while physical decay and derelict land have severely detrimental effects on it. In addition, physical environment is expected to play an important role in city marketing by providing a material expression to the city images that city branding attempts to create. For example, the image of a city as a "vibrant" and "cosmopolitan" place that city branding is trying to deliver can be realised in the physical form of the buildings and public places that visitors encounter in the city. The use of architecture for city branding is sometimes called "hard-branding", and has become an important feature in place marketing.

2. URBAN ENTREPRENEURIALISM AND POLICIES TO MAKE CITIES ATTRACTIVE

Physical environment has posed major challenges for planners who attempt to restructure the economies of former industrial cities, which declined steadily throughout the latter half of the 20th century. Their declining image was not just an image but a physical reality of dereliction and decay. Hence, in order to change their images, planners had to address the physical problems first. This was the basic strategy in the revitalisation of Bilbao, which is regarded as one of the prime examples of urban regeneration through physical renovation (see Box 2.1).

Box 2.1. **Strategic plan to revitalise Bilbao**

Physical renovation was a key element in the strategic plans to revitalise the Bilbao metropolitan area, which had declined steadily since the end of the 1970s. First, urban planners developed a new vision of the city as a post-industrial city that would secure its place among world-class metropolitan centres.

Second, in order to achieve economic revitalisation based on the new vision, planners thought it essential to replace the city's negative image of deindustrialisation and decline with a new image of a better-looking, innovative, attractive city.

Third, planners decided that the change in image could be achieved through transformation of the city's physical environment and the use of aggressive place-marketing campaigns. This strategic thinking acted as the basis for large emblematic projects and riverfront redevelopment, such as the Guggenheim Museum and the Bilbao International Exhibition Centre. The authorities commissioned these projects to internationally famed architects to ensure that they stood out as symbols of modernity and renaissance, and that they could be featured in place-marketing campaigns.

Fourth, the strategies had a conspicuous bias toward the downtown area, where abandoned industrial sites and derelict waterfront areas were concentrated. This area, which was close to the central business district, was considered an "opportunity area" with high potential for commercial property development.

Thus, the physical renovation of the city centre area was considered a vital element to enhance the city's image and restructure its economy. This strategy, which makes physical renovation of the city centre a key element of urban development, has become a common feature of urban regeneration programmes in many other cities, particularly old industrial cities.

Source: Vicario, L. and P. M. Martínez Monje (2003), "Another 'Guggenheim Effect'? The Generation of a Potentially Gentrifiable Neighbourhood in Bilbao", Urban Studies, Vol. 40, No. 12, pp. 2383-2400.

In efforts to physically renovate city environments, much attention has been directed to city centres because they serve as focal points for urban life, and often contain important social and cultural heritage, making them the most conspicuous elements in the physical attractiveness of a city. Hence, city centres have often been chosen as the most strategic locations for policy planners to concentrate limited public resources to enhance city attractiveness, and since the midst of the 1980s' property-boom, large-scale physical redevelopment of city centres took centre stage in the process of enhancing city image (Hall and Hubbard, 1998).

The waterfront plays a crucial role in urban spatial development because it is usually close to the city centre and "water" is an important element in an attractive urban environment. However, in the industrial cities of the 19th and 20th centuries, it was almost exclusively allocated to industrial use, and the general public was denied access to it. Although the structural economic change was itself a major policy challenge for urban economic planners, industrial restructuring was, from the standpoint of urban land use, an opportunity to liberate waterfront land for new uses. In other words, it opened up new opportunities to use urban resources for broader objectives.

The question was to what land use the waterfront should be converted. The dominant solution has been to use it to build new city images, based on the recognition of its strategic importance in urban space. This has led to the proliferation of a particular type of city centre redevelopment project, called "flagship redevelopment", with distinctive characteristics. These redevelopments are meant to be the "signature" of the city and embody the images developed in strategic visions for city promotion.

What provided the worldwide model for the strategic use of flagship developments on the waterfront for city promotion were waterfront developments in the United States, particularly in Baltimore and Boston (see Box 2.2). These models paved the way for the proliferation on a global scale of waterfront developments, based on these two examples. The extent of the Baltimore model's influence varies from one city to another. In some cases, such as the Darling Harbour in Sydney, its direct influence is fairly evident, whereas in others, the scale of the development considerably exceeds that of the Baltimore project, as in the case of the London Docklands development, which covers an area of 22 km^2. There are also cases, such as the Old Port of Barcelona, which achieved a unique redevelopment although it incorporated many elements from the Baltimore model (Ward, 2002). The size of the cities where the waterfront developments are located also varies considerably, ranging from worldwide financial centres, such as New York, London and Tokyo, to cities that are regional centres.

> ## Box 2.2. **The Baltimore Model**
>
> For most of its history, Baltimore's economy has been dominated by its port and by industry. The city and its surrounding area benefited from its location in the important corridor along the northeast coast of the United States between Philadelphia and Washington and from an overflow of federal government and linked activities from Washington. The decline of the city was caused primarily by two factors. First, as is the case in other American cities, the decentralisation of many activities to the suburbs brought about the overall decline of the core, and second, the increasing use of containers in ships and the growing size of the ships have necessitated the movement of port activities downstream and led to the abandonment of old harbours, including the city's Inner Harbor. Consequently, many of the old waterfront industries located there have also closed down.
>
> The efforts to reverse the decline of the city started in the 1950s, when the decay of the downtown area became apparent to the public. The initiative was taken by the private sector, such as retailers and the leading business people in the area. They commissioned a plan for the central area, which was subsequently submitted to the mayor and city council and was accepted by them in 1959 when work on the plan started. The initial project centred on the quarter that was later named the Charles Center project, which consisted mainly of offices, although there was also a theatre, civic centre, hotel, and residential block.
>
> The success of the initial project paved the way for another project in the Inner Harbor, where the departure of trade had left an empty, derelict and often unsafe area. In 1965, a plan was drawn up which provided for substantial redevelopment on the waterfront, including a park, housing and some offices. Later in the 1970s, the remodeling of the Inner Harbor was considered and several tourist sites were introduced, such as a museum, the Maryland Science Center (1976), a convention centre (1979), a festival marketplace called Harbor Place (1980), the National Aquarium and the Hyatt Hotel (1981). The US Constellation, built in 1797, was moored in the harbor in 1972, and later, other ships were also brought in to create a maritime museum. The first stage of the remodeling of the Inner Harbor was completed by 1981, and the area soon acquired a worldwide reputation as a successful example of waterfront development. Policy planners and academics around the world flocked to Baltimore to look at the spectacular transformation of the Inner Harbor, which later came to be known as the Baltimore Model.
>
> Source: Law, C. M. (1993), *Urban Tourism: Attracting Visitors to Large Cities*, Mansell Publishing, London.

Flagship city centre developments share some common characteristics. First of all, physically they are large-scale, so that they have significant impacts on city image. They have high profiles because they feature innovative designs by internationally-famed architects. The use of internationally-known professionals has also been essential for securing the financing necessary for such developments.

Second, private investment was eagerly sought to finance the developments, and the extent of the success of the projects was often measured by such criteria as leverage ratios. In most cases, investors' decisions were made based on expectations of the project's potential as a property development, and, thus, such projects assumed the nature of property-led developments. In order to secure the project's potential as a property development, project locations were carefully chosen so that their economic potential could be realised with minimum public investment in infrastructure improvements.

Third, planning controls were often made flexible to encourage private investment. For example, special planning procedures were granted for the developments in enterprise zones in the United Kingdom (such as Canary Wharf in the London Docklands), where planning control was restricted to outline controls and planning procedures were in the hands of the Urban Development Corporation, which is a pro-development central government organisation, instead of the local authorities, whose procedures were generally regarded as time-consuming and inflexible. These measures aimed at overcoming supply-side constraints on property development by streamlining the planning system, and speeding up the process of land-acquisition and assembly (Healey, 1991).

These prestigious projects, which often require a considerable amount of public and private investment, are expected to act as symbols of urban regeneration based on modern and dynamic economies. Indeed, in many successful cases, they had significant impact on urban economic regeneration. For example, Canary Wharf in the London Docklands, together with other deregulatory changes in the financial and stock markets, considerably contributed to the strengthening of London's status as a world-class financial centre. However, it has been pointed out that private developers, especially international developers, are not particularly interested in developments in cities at the lower end of the scale of the urban hierarchy, such as regional and provincial centres (Ward, 2002). This shows that projects are very much dependent on the economic potential of the project location or of the city where they are located.

Another important characteristic of flagship developments is that they are multiple-land-use developments with residential, office, commercial, entertainment and leisure uses. They are also strongly characterised by land use for the consumption of the types of urban services and cultures that appeal to the highly-qualified professionals and creative workers who are the primary targets of city promotion. It is assumed that the extension of consumerism into all areas of private and social life, including art, leisure and pleasure, has brought about a situation where it constitutes an important factor in the quality of urban life, particularly for knowledge workers, and that a city should be well equipped with these functions in order to present itself as an attractive place for these people to live and work. The so-called festival market, which is a common feature in many waterfront developments, represents this idea. Similarly, residential developments strongly reflect the preferences of these people.

It is undeniable that successful flagship developments have produced remarkable achievements, demonstrated by impressive urban landscapes that have materialised on sites which used to be rundown areas with a concentration of economic, social and environmental problems. Appropriate property developments provided the physical platform for a comprehensive programme intended to achieve all-round regeneration. Therefore, it is fair to say that property-led regeneration constitutes a necessary component of urban revitalisation, particularly when the impact of economic restructuring necessitates the land-use conversion of large tracts of derelict land.

However, it has also become apparent that flagship developments are neither sufficient nor adequate for urban regeneration of wider areas. It has even been argued that their effect has been divisive and marginal and that many cities have become more unequal in the last 20 years (Imrie and Thomas, 1993). It is sometimes the case that links between these projects and existing local economies are weak and that they are reduced to closed economic enclaves detached from the wider local economic fabric. For example, in spite of the remarkable success of the waterfront development in Baltimore, which was attracting 22 million visitors annually by the late 1980s, and has provided the template for subsequent waterfront developments worldwide, economic and social problems persist in areas that are at a distance of just a few blocks (Ward, 2002). The mayor of the city was obliged to conclude that conditions in most of the city's neighbourhoods had become worse in the "renaissance years" (Hambleton, 1991).

1.3. Culture-led and event-driven urban regeneration

Although cultural elements were sometimes included in public urban intervention, they have generally been adopted essentially as a welfare service, in which the main concern was to provide wider social groups with access to an artistic and cultural heritage, and opportunities to express themselves in the society (Griffiths, 1995). Later, by linking cultural elements to city promotion, they acquired a status as a strategic tool for city promotion and are increasingly becoming an essential component in urban economic regeneration policies for multiple reasons. First, they are regarded as an effective tool to boost urban tourism, which generates spending and creates jobs, in the hope that a substantial number of jobs would be created indirectly by cultural investment in the form of jobs that serve visitors and audiences in restaurants, shops and hotels. The increasing dependence of the economy on tourism is driving this trend further (Griffiths, 1993). This is particularly the case in the former industrial cities, which have lost a considerable number of jobs, especially unskilled jobs, in the course of economic restructuring. It is hoped that tourism-related service sectors will provide job opportunities for them.

Another reason is the widely-perceived potential of cultural elements in enhancing city image and attractiveness. In fact, in many successful cases where considerable enhancement and improvement of city image were achieved, so-called "culture-led" policies were a central feature in the strategies. Behind this was a widely-shared assumption that culture possesses a strong attracting power over highly-skilled and creative workers, and that attempts to persuade these people to locate in certain cities will be aided if they are associated with arts, culture and entertainment. Cultural infrastructure, such as theatres, museums, and galleries, acts as a powerful magnet for creative people by offering attractive lifestyle opportunities. There is some empirical evidence to support this assumption. For example, the survey by the Kommunalverband Ruhr showed that 69% of the managers interviewed regarded urban cultural facilities as an important contribution to the image and quality of life of a city, and that companies in the services sector have a stronger tendency to view "culture" as an important location factor, with 50% of them viewing culture positively, as opposed to 30% of the companies in the secondary sector (Skrodzki, 1989).

Cultural investment is also thought to contribute to the diversification of the local economic base by sowing the seeds of new economic sectors that could eventually grow into major growth engines in knowledge economies. For this strategy, production, rather than consumption, of culture is emphasized. New cultural infrastructure, such as galleries, theatres and concert halls, is expected to play a role, not only as a tourist attraction, but also as a community platform for culture-related economies to expand.

Culture-led urban regeneration policy played a crucial role in many city centre renovation projects, where cultural facilities constitute a central part of the flagship redevelopment. An example is the Massachusetts Museum of Contemporary Art and Architecture, the world's largest museum of contemporary art, opened in 1993 on a site that was occupied by an industrial plant until 1986. It is an enormous museum complex that incorporates massive cultural spaces together with shops and restaurants, aiming at becoming a new attraction for mass tourism and entertainment (Griffiths, 1993).

The role of cultural communities in urban gentrification has long been known to policy planners. It has been observed that in the process of urban gentrification, where areas that were formerly decayed are rehabilitated gradually and spontaneously, the existence of "urban pioneers", who act as early-stage gentrifiers, plays a crucial role. Such people include various types of artists and creative workers, who initially form a seminal agglomeration. In successful cases, it grows into a full-fledged expansion of cultural activities, reinforcing the agglomeration process by being more distinctive and identifiable and thus attracting still more creative people.

Cultural clusters are an effort to trigger such a process by conscious planning (see Box 2.3). Although the famous cultural quarters were actually never planned as such, and developed more or less spontaneously, it was envisaged that the planned creation of agglomerations of cultural activities would produce a similar climate and initiate the self-reinforcing process of attracting creative people to the area. In many cases of planned cultural clusters, not only arts and cultures but also various leisure and entertainment facilities, such as bars, restaurants and health and fitness centres are also included. Although the extent to which these elements are mixed varies from project to project, many of them are distinctively consumption-oriented, which reflects the crucial role they are expected to play in place marketing, directed particularly at knowledge workers. Cultural elements are positioned in the context of imagery or branding strategy to give prestige or spatial identity to the location.

In recent years, there has been a growing awareness of the economic potential of hosting major events for urban regeneration. It is believed that major events provide excellent opportunities for city marketing by attracting national and international attention and considerable numbers of people, who can then have a first-hand experience of the city. Most city promoters think that an actual visit to the city is highly effective in overcoming the limitations inherent in city marketing, such as regional stereotypes and public doubt about its impartiality.

Major events, particularly international events, such as the Olympic Games and World EXPO, also attach prestige to the host city and raise its profile on the international stage. This recognition has been driving many cities to earnestly seek such opportunities, and the concept of "event city" has come to be known to policy makers as describing the fact that an event can be used to give a special character to the city that hosts it, change its image, and thus change the local economy. Major events, particularly on an international

> ## Box 2.3. **Cultural clusters**
>
> When cultural facilities form a complex, combining a mixture of cultural functions and activities, they are called "cultural clusters", and the planned creation of them has been rapidly becoming an important component of culture-led urban regeneration. Although they take different spatial forms, from stand-alone buildings or larger building complexes to entire quarters or networks of locations, they are basically planned geographical concentrations of functions that share a cultural image and identity.
>
> Cultural clusters were inspired by such agglomerations as 1900 Montmartre, 1960s Rive Gauche, 1970s SoHo, where dense concentration of cultural activities provided local climates favourable for creative activities to flourish. This, in turn, further strengthened the attractiveness of the place, and thus effectively created a virtuous cycle. The strong tendency of cultural activities to agglomerate in specific places has been a target of academic interest and it is thought that the symbolic character of the products and services produced requires marketing tactics that make use of the brand or identity, which a successful cultural cluster can attach to the place. The symbolic value of a cultural cluster is said to provide a market advantage for the cultural products and services that are associated with the place. The key for successful cultural clusters is whether their locations can amass a critical mixture of spatial, professional and cultural qualities with which creative people want to associate themselves.
>
> Mommaas (2004) lists, as examples of a cultural cluster, such places as the Temple Bar area in Dublin, the Museums Quarter in Vienna, the Custard Factory in Birmingham, the fashion and textile quarter of Ticinese in Milan, the late-19th century textile factory chain of Finish Tampere, the network of industrial landmark projects in NordRhein Westfalen, the multimedia cluster of Hoxton in London, or the Lowly Centre complex in Salford, together with four Dutch examples of consciously-planned cultural clusters, namely the Museum Quarter in Rotterdam, the Westergasfabriek in Amsterdam, the Veemarktkwartier in Tilburg and the Museum and Theatre Quarter in Utrecht.
>
> Source: Mommaas, H. (2004), "Cultural Clusters and the Post-industrial City: Towards the Remapping of Urban Cultural Policy", *Urban Studies*, Vol. 41, No. 3.

scale, are an opportunity for the host city to achieve international prominence, enhance its image and hence promote physical and economic regeneration.

Hosting a major event also has a significant impact on improvement of the physical environment of the city that hosts it. Investment in infrastructure, such as airports, public transport, road networks, hotel accommodation, water and sewage systems and urban landscaping, is necessary to ensure the effective operation of an event and to exploit the full potential of city marketing it provides by presenting the best possible image of the city to visitors. Such events also leave a considerable legacy that can provide an important foundation for future economic development. Major events act as a catalyst to secure the public consensus on putting these investments on the fast-track by attaching first priority to public expenditure programmes. This has particularly been the case when such major events appealed to local or even national aspirations.

A case in point is the Tokyo Olympic Games of 1964, which were the first Olympic Games in Asia and symbolised the post-war reconstruction of Japan. The Games were used positively as an impetus to accelerate implementation of the urban development plan of Tokyo, which laid out the foundation for subsequent development of Tokyo, and involved a wide range of infrastructure investment, comprising substantial improvements in the system of urban highways and in water management systems. Barcelona is a city that used major international events as a means to enhance its attractiveness, by using these "hallmark" events as a trigger for various urban improvements, thus providing a stimulus to the work of planners, architects and artists. For example, the city used the 1992 Olympic Games as a catalyst for urban renovation by changing urban structures and creating public open space which had already been proposed in 1980, long before its hosting. The Olympic Games contributed to bringing forward many public investment schemes which might otherwise have been implemented much later. The catalytic influence of major international events to accelerate infrastructure improvements has also been evident in many other cases.

It is noteworthy that many of these events were not intended to perform roles in urban economic regeneration when they were originally conceived, and that their potential for urban economic regeneration was astutely identified and exploited by policy planners. In some cases, technological advancements, notably the advent of global media-coverage and transport, significantly increased their economic potential for urban regeneration. The most significant case is perhaps the Olympic Games. While the television rights for the 1960 Olympic Games in Rome were purchased for USD 440 000, those for the 1996 Atlanta Games were sold for USD 900 million. The rights for the Games in 2008 in Beijing have been purchased for USD 3.6 billion (Chalkley and Essex, 1999). This surge in global media interest in the Olympic Games has strengthened significantly their influence on the economic regeneration of the city which hosts them.

Some issues have arisen in culture and event policies for urban regeneration. It has been argued that linking cultural policy to urban regeneration may sometimes have detrimental effects on local cultural development, particularly if precious public resources are diverted from existing cultural policies to prestigious cultural projects. For example, some prestigious cultural projects were made possible at the expense of substantial cuts in the budgets for education and culture. It has also been pointed out that, in many cases, their consumption – instead of production – oriented nature prohibited them from acting as catalysts for developing spontaneous local cultural activities that could eventually grow into new industries (Mommaas, 2004). "Functionalisation" of culture for the purpose of boosting urban tourism and consumption and exploiting its potential for city promotion may, it is argued, have negative effects on the development of local cultural activities by favouring "safe", unchallenging works and by marginalising other, sometimes more critical, voices (Griffiths, 1995). This could have prohibitive effects on the development of local culture with a strong identity and distinctive characteristics, like those of 1960s Rive Gauche and 1970s SoHo, where cultural activities developed spontaneously.

2. Key issues: overcoming urban policy dilemmas

Griffiths (1995) argues that the use of cultural policies as a tool for urban economic regeneration brought about strategic dilemmas for policy planners that sometimes caused deep tension in local communities over the question of how such strategies for urban regeneration should be used. The first dilemma is which audience should be targeted: whether urban regeneration should be directed towards outside audiences, such as corporate investors and the mobile workforce, or towards serving the local population's needs and strengthening their identity and self-confidence. The second dilemma is related to geographical focus: whether priority should be placed on the city centre, which possesses a strategic location advantage for the purpose of city promotion, or on the neighbourhoods where citizens live. The third dilemma is related to what economic activities such strategies should promote: whether strategies should target consumption, which plays a crucial role in the quality of life of highly-qualified urban professionals and the creative workforce who are usually targeted by city promotion, or production, which will provide new economic staples for the urban economy. The fourth dilemma is the choice between facilities and activities: whether precious public resources should be directed towards investment in new permanent buildings and spaces, or toward supporting activities.

In the face of these tactical problems, it is possible to identify broader urban policy agenda which often demand apparently contradictory considerations. They are the key issues posing difficult choices for policy planners who share the concern that policies to enhance city attractiveness should be employed in such a manner that would strengthen social cohesion in the city, because these issues are, in one way or another, related to the problem of how to reconcile the strategic approach and social cohesion. Social cohesion is one of the most fundamental bases for cities to be attractive and competitive, as well as a precondition for strategic urban regeneration programmes to be accepted by the communities and implemented with the commitment and collaboration of a wide range of local stakeholders. Therefore, it is crucial to overcome these key issues, if such policies are to maintain long-term viability in the urban civic society and achieve urban regeneration. Such efforts would require a new policy approach that is innovative and inclusive.

2.1. Globalisation and localisation

It is often pointed out that the conflicting trends of globalisation and localisation are influencing urban spatial development policy planning at the same time (OECD, 2005). Each of them has different policy implications, which are often pointing in opposite directions. This may be due to the fact that localisation is understood partly as a counter-movement to globalisation, which inevitably has homogenising effects on locations. City attractiveness necessarily reflects both elements; a city should meet the sort of global standards that multinational firms and mobile talents demand if they are to attract them by the city's promotion. On the other hand, distinctive local identity is an essential element in distinguishing a city on the global market.

However, what has emerged from past experience of policies to enhance attractiveness is an ironic situation where such policies have, in many cases, ended up undermining the local distinctiveness and uniqueness that a city originally possessed, and brought about homogeneous identities of many global cities. Local identity is often glossed over in an attempt to present a city as a slick retail and recreation location. Only those aspects of its heritage that are considered internationally-saleable are celebrated and marketed (McGuirk, et al., 1998).

Flagship city centre developments, composed of a formulaic mix of commercial, residential, leisure and industrial uses, have often been described as "analogous cities" because of the way they accommodate office workers, tourists and conference visitors in an almost identical physical space which is sanitised of traditional street life (Boddy, 1992). For instance, it is widely known that a successful model of waterfront development in Baltimore has been copied by many urban planners in various countries and has appeared in virtually every city with developable waterfront space, sharing similar features such as an aquarium, waterside promenades, festival market places, restored ships, converted warehouses, and so on. This has resulted in a paradoxical situation where everywhere seems like everywhere else (Boyer, 1992).

Similarly, museums, which played a leading role in culture-led policies, have become a common factor to such an extent that in Britain it was estimated that during the 1980s new museums were opening at the rate of one a fortnight (Griffiths, 1993). With virtually all major cities having museums, this type of cultural policy caused a severe oversupply of cultural facilities in major cities, and they are hardly a distinguishing factor for attractiveness anymore.

In event-driven policies, similar problems have arisen. In accordance with the extent to which cultural policies are integrated into place marketing, "safer" and more consumption-oriented cultural contents are selected, marginalising local indigenous cultural activities.

Place marketing originally aimed at differentiating a city from others on the global market. However, what happened was that the globally-oriented urban entrepreneurialism often emaciated local identity and replaced it with repetitious mass-produced images to the point where it is hardly possible to distinguish a newly-created physical environment from many others. What is urgently required for policy planners to do is to integrate both globalisation and localisation in spatial development strategies, such as flagship developments and cultural clusters, so that a unique combination of the two perspectives enhances the distinctiveness and identity that a city already possesses. Such efforts could be achieved by careful planning that incorporates both a visual image of exciting and dynamic urban environments and a higher standard of quality of life, and the local identity rooted in citizens' aspirations. Physical expression of the historical origins of a city plays a crucial role for citizens to feel an affinity with a new landscape materialised by redevelopment projects. It is also an important element to get citizens' support and participation, and could only be achieved by paying careful attention to the cultural and historical assets a city possesses. Cultural and historical heritage have not always been distinctively featured in past city centre development projects. Even if historical features were included, they were sometimes out of the local context, as in the case of historical ships that were added to many waterfront developments. Careful attention should be paid to local historical context as an essential ingredient of the new urban landscape.

The integration of globalisation and localisation requires an innovative approach which identifies and mobilises the unnoticed assets and potential a city possesses. Such innovativeness of urban entrepreneurialism was vividly demonstrated by the early policy pioneers who vigorously sought out and experimented with new policy tools. Their hidden potential was astutely identified and effectively harnessed as an important strategic tool. Unfortunately, the subsequent tendency of policy planners to rely heavily on a small number of successful cases as "good practices" sometimes resulted in inadequate efforts to develop creative strategies that pay careful consideration to the historical context and local assets every city possesses.

Certain factors could be responsible for this situation. First of all, the strong orientation towards place marketing inevitably tends to favour the groups of people that such strategies try to attract. Thus, the newly-created built-environment would be designed to appeal to the stereotyped tastes of the groups of people that planners envisaged in their place marketing as the target audience: highly-qualified urban professionals who engage in knowledge activities. Consequently, strong similarities among localities would emerge.

Second, the marketing of cities is done largely by local government officials without specialist advertising training. Consequently, their methods tend to be generic and repetitive (Holcomb, 1994). It was also pointed out that the degree of freedom of local government officials, who work within the framework of best practice, best value and statutory responsibilities, is considerably restricted. When these policies are not backed by strong political leadership, planners tend to avoid taking risks by not deviating from much-acclaimed success cases, such as the Baltimore model (Chatterton and Unsworth, 2004).

Third, local governments suffering from perpetual funding shortfalls are under heavy pressure to maximise the revenue from land disposals. Such harsh realities of stringent budgets and preoccupation with public debt inevitably result in the priority of investment-return over other considerations, and consequently picking development proposals that will realise the best commercial value. This situation, which could be described as lack of effective public ownership of physical space to be used for urban revitalisation, results in the inability of local governments to do more than simply specify what will be acceptable on the project site (Chatterton and Unsworth, 2004).

Similarly, property developers, which undertake renovation projects based on loans from banks and have responsibility to shareholders, prioritise the financial returns from the project site which they usually acquire at a high cost by open tendering. This "bottom line" profit motive makes it very difficult for property developers to accept riskier development plans. Thus, a strong commonality occurs among a number of projects, which tends to consist of a similar set of architectural and land use elements. These financial constraints compel both public and private sectors to put a priority on predictability by adopting a safer line.

From these observations it is apparent that what is necessary to overcome these difficulties and achieve diverse strategies is the strong leadership that enables policy planners to take calculated risks and adopt innovative approaches. Policy innovation cannot be obtained without the courage to experiment.

2.2. Market and community

The second issue is the relationship between the market and the community. The entrepreneurial approach towards urban economic regeneration aims essentially at exploiting market forces to the maximum through such measures as private investment, urban marketing, deregulation and new institutional mechanisms (public-private partnership, development agencies, etc.) Indeed, private firms have been playing an increasingly important role in strategic projects for city promotion with their financial resources and management expertise. Therefore, many policy planners, quite rightly, pay a great deal of attention to creating the best conditions for private investment. The role of private investment should, and will continue to increase in future, too, and there still remains much that policy planners can do to promote it.

However, despite the overall nature of such projects as market-driven and privately-initiated, their success still very much depends on public investment and intervention, such as transport infrastructure provision, land acquisition and assembly, subsidies and tax incentives. This was most evident in the development of waterfront areas, which are quite often equipped with poor local access for historical reasons.* Therefore, considerable investment in transport is necessary to change their image of isolation. For example, the take-off of the Canary Wharf in the London Docklands as the second financial centre in London was partially but crucially supported by the extension of the London Underground to the area and the upgrading of the road connection to central London. Also, in the change of land use from low-density industrial use to higher-density mixed use that consists of commercial and residential uses, large sums of capital are necessary to invest in upgrading basic infrastructure, because the block sizes, street locations, access points, utility capacity and street widths become inappropriate for the new land uses.

The necessary public investment often amounts to a considerable sum. The rationale behind investing such a significant amount of public resources in specific projects is that they contribute to addressing wider policy objectives. Therefore, policy goals and private interests should be carefully co-ordinated so that both can benefit from the other. Public-private partnership is the institutional framework where such co-ordination takes place. However, in some cases, concerns were expressed that excessive preoccupation with securing as much private capital as possible in the short term could result in a

* Older port facilities are said to be deliberately designed to be inaccessible to discourage theft and smuggling and vehicular movement (Gordon, 1996).

shift of balance towards private interests, which is manifest in the situation where the success of strategic projects is gauged principally by such criteria as leverage ratios. This gives the impression that public interests are being neglected, while precious public money is being spent for private purposes and the public-private partnership has become an institution simply to serve private interests.

The problem is aggravated by the nature of investment strategies adopted for urban economic regeneration. Strategic investment is, from policy planners' viewpoint, essential to reverse the continuing decline and erosion of the economic base, and "strategic" usually means the concentration of investment on key projects, whether they are flagship city centre developments, cultural facilities or hosting major events. This entrepreneurial approach was proposed to the public with the promise of improvements in overall social welfare by bringing the local population into sync with the demands of a globalised economy, based on the premise that the strategic concentration of investment eventually brings about economic effects on wider areas, which are described as "trickle down effects".

However, concentration of precious public resources on a small number of selected projects has often caused strong criticism from citizens who feel they were "left out" of the process. Such locations are usually selected based on their potential as commercial property developments, and consequently located in the city centres. The concentration of public money on areas that already have significant economic advantages appears, in the eyes of the general public, as unfair. Situations where such locations are subsequently occupied by the urban rich after the final land use is realised fuels such criticism. For example, in Frankfurt, which attracted the interest of urban policy planners with its spectacular cultural investment, political and social opposition was expressed against it on the grounds that only the "new urban middle classes" and wealthy outsiders, not the "average Frankfurter", benefited from it, and that it deepened social conflicts (Friedrichs, and Dangshat, 1993). In fact, in stark contrast to the massive cultural investment, the budget for neighbourhood-based culture was cut back in 1988.

Similar criticisms have been directed against hosting major international events, which has been increasingly perceived as extravagant by the general public. It is ironic that the increase in the scale of the events, which contributes to the increased opportunities for city image enhancement, has also increasingly invited public opposition. For example, some cities met strong local hostility to hosting Olympic Games because the ordinary population questioned the appropriateness of the huge public investment required to stage the Games while severe social problems, which also require public investment, still remained. Strong public opposition sometimes forced governments to scale down planned investment in infrastructure, which could otherwise have provided an important foundation for a city's long-term development. The risk of long-term indebtedness resulting from hosting major events has also fuelled opposition against it.

Such a situation is particularly detrimental for strategic projects because citizens' support is the precondition for such projects to have long-term viability in the urban civic society. Strong local opposition makes it difficult to fully exploit the opportunities that such projects provide, as has been demonstrated in many cases. However, the public investment involved in such strategic projects would not necessarily cause local tension. For example, such strategic projects would not be regarded as created at the sacrifice of local communities if they were financed by tapping into new resources rather than diverting the existing budget allocated to local communities. The following approaches could also be adopted to create conditions so that the local population thinks that their interests and needs are being duly reflected and feel a sense of ownership in such projects.

2.2.1. A visible link with quality of life

Firstly, citizens need to see a visible link between such projects and an increase in the quality of daily life in order to feel a sense of ownership in such projects. Achieving this would require a change in policy planning approach from the view, taken for granted in traditional place marketing, that city attractiveness should be appreciated from the perspective of an outside audience which is its potential target, to the notion that the quality of life of citizens forms the core of city attractiveness (OECD, 2005). The previous approach would give an impression to local communities that their interests were being neglected. Strategies should be built on the premise that city attractiveness has its basis in the quality of life of its citizens.

The physical environment is the most visible result of urban regeneration, and has significant implications for citizens' lives. Its inclusiveness and openness provide the basis for the social and cultural vibrancy of the city. They also have economic implications. For example, consumption-oriented cultural venues could contribute to encouraging and promoting local cultural production if it is not excluded but positively consumed in such venues. They could demonstrate that consumption and production are two sides of the same coin that can complement each other, rather than be viewed as a policy dilemma.

In this regard, public space plays a crucial role. It is the physical expression of the inclusiveness that the strategic approaches for urban regeneration are based on. It not only contributes to social cohesion by providing a milieu for citizens' social life but also helps local cultural production to manifest itself by providing cultural venues accessible to local artists who have limited access to the upper-market cultural venues in the city centre. It is widely accepted that the cultural vibrancy in many continental European cities, such as Brussels, is underpinned by the existence of large public open spaces in the city centres.

However, the effectiveness of public spaces in stimulating vibrant social life and diverse cultural creativity is predicated on their "openness". It is said that the emergence of leisure economies and predominance of consumerism in every aspect of urban life has brought about a phenomenon of "privatisation of public space" (McNeill and While, 2001), which can be observed in many physical renovation projects with cultural and leisure facilities only for people with considerable disposable income. It can manifest in the form of managed shopping environments and defensive design strategies, which are exclusionary to those who are not the envisaged target as consumers of the types of goods and services they provide. Hence, restoring public space, which is accessible, enjoyable and psychologically welcoming, is an effective measure to counteract this trend.

2.2.2. Inclusive process

There is a growing recognition, not only in the public sector but also in the private sector, that securing citizens' support by getting them involved in the development process increases the predictability and certainty of projects (OECD, 2005). In fact, past experience shows that one of the most difficult tasks for policy planners in adopting entrepreneurialism is to secure the support and commitment of the existing residents for their strategic approach. Such support is crucial for the long-term viability of such policies, and it is becoming a widespread understanding that an inclusive process in strategy planning is a necessary condition, if not always sufficient. It gives a democratic legitimacy to the strategies produced, and provides a fair chance to reflect and co-ordinate various and often conflicting interests in the communities. It provides important opportunities for diverse interests and policy dilemmas to be reconciled by effective and active participation. Participants in such an open process would regard the strategies produced as their own production rather that what is simply delivered by the politicians and public officials for them to accept.

Public-private partnership has been long-established as a key element in entrepreneurial metropolitan governance. Although such partnership, in many cases, consists of very diverse interest groups, it is still not always the case that such partnership reaches out to citizens and civic society, beyond the local business circle. Information dissemination to the general public becomes a fairly common practice, but integrating them in the planning and implementation process is still rare.

Explaining such a situation, it is sometimes argued that difficulties exist in engaging local residents in strategic planning because the interests of local communities quite often do not go beyond the vicinity of their neighbourhoods. Their strong inclination to preserve the status quo often makes it very difficult to think strategically to harness the economic potential of the area for wider benefits. In order to overcome such difficulties, the capacity-building of local communities for strategic thinking is essential. Inclusive and participatory planning processes would contribute to it by providing local residents with opportunities to share the policy planners' perspectives, and to engage in policy discussion in the course of strategy planning. Such exposure can enhance the residents' perspectives of the policy issues surrounding their city and contribute to build up their capacity for strategic thinking beyond their local interests.

Difficulties also exist with regard to local representation. Over the decades, substantial cases have been accumulated where community groups had direct involvement in urban regeneration. The case of Coin Street in London, United Kingdom, where a community-led scheme has eventually been implemented, is a prominent case. However, in other cases, true local representation is not necessarily guaranteed by an institutional framework created spontaneously by local residents. Strong community action is often based on socially and ethnically homogeneous neighbourhoods, with the risk of excluding vulnerable groups at the margin (Deakin and Edwards, 1993). There is also a risk of having local representation hijacked by pressure groups with policy agendas which do not necessarily reflect the communities' interests. Hence, it is essential to have an institutional framework by which the interests of the community are truly represented.

In addition, even when the importance of involving a wide range of stakeholders from the vision creation stage is well-appreciated, some pitfalls exist. For example, by rushing to obtain a consensus with the backing of many stakeholders, strategic visions sometimes end up being just a series of safe objectives that do not offend established interests and reflect the lowest-common-denominator, a list of projects and an institutional mechanism (Griffiths, 1995). However, a strategy that does not clearly define the content of the image that it is seeking to construct for the city does not constitute a strategy. This is most likely to occur when the institutional mechanism to involve a wide range of stakeholders is remote from any effective public or private sector power and when there is no effective leadership with adequate institutional capacity (Griffiths, 1995).

2.2.3. *Investment information for market transparency*

The balance between public and private interests could only be achieved when both public and private sectors can work on an equal basis, and if the stage is tilted to either of them, a balance should be restored. Such a situation typically occurs when the position of local governments is relatively weak in the public-private partnership because outside investors' interest is rather weak due to the widespread assumption that investment return in such areas would be unrewarding. If such an assumption does not properly reflect the reality, it is a market failure that could be corrected by information.

Property investment is inherently a risky business, and investors' strong propensity to minimise risk propels them to direct their property investment decisions to narrowly-defined areas of a limited number of world cities. The comparative availability of investment information in such cities, and conversely lack of such information in less-favoured areas, accelerates this tendency. Therefore, positive dissemination of investment information could contribute to outside-investor awareness of the opportunities if an objective and statistical case can be made for them. For example, in the United Kingdom, the government, in conjunction with the private sector, produced a statistical comparison which shows that property investment in inner cities can produce higher investment returns than property investment in general (OECD, 2005). This approach can have significant implications for the way in which city promotion is conducted because it has not necessarily been the case that such objective information dissemination has been given enough attention. Attractive narratives and images are an important part of city promotion. However, sober investment decisions are still very much dependent on objective information. It provides the basis for the market to function optimally, and also contribute to the strengthening of the bargaining position of local communities.

2.3. Long-term and short-term goals

There is a different degree of emphasis between long-term and short-term goals. If economic regeneration is conceived as a process of re-building local economies into those with strong competitive advantages relative to new global economic trends, it should address structural issues in local economies. However, the urgency of social and economic problems that industrial decline poses for policy planners unavoidably compels them to aim at conspicuous gains in the shortest time. The growing share and importance in urban regeneration projects of private money, for which predictability is an essential condition, also leads to a demand for returns in a fixed period of time. Such a short-term emphasis is particularly apparent in the nature of land use materialised after physical renovation, which is strongly characterised by urban consumption.

Long-term and short-term goals are not necessarily exclusive; but are usually closely connected in strategic planning. It is anticipated that long-term economic effects will follow short-term impacts in the form of "trickle down" or "spill over" effects. Short-term emphasis, it is thought, is necessary to produce a critical mass, which subsequently initiates a long-term and self-sustaining process of economic re-structuring.

However, while growth-promoting entrepreneurial strategies have facilitated the revitalisation of the built-environment of many inner cities, and contributed to the creation of new images and economic recovery in many former industrial cities, empirical evidence from the studies of a number of cities in the United States and western Europe has repeatedly suggested that urban entrepreneurial strategies have not lived up to their promises by demonstrating effectiveness in addressing the long-standing problems of urban communities (Leitner and Sheppard, 1998). In the worst cases, it has been argued, such a strategic approach to urban regeneration is aggravating social divisions by effectively creating a dual city of "haves" and "have nots", with deprived or community groups gaining little or nothing from the regeneration process (Jones, 1998). It is often the case that new gentrified spaces are found only a few hundred metres from some of the most deprived areas of inner-city decay, characterised by chronic dependency, poverty and frequent social unrest (Hall and Hubbard, 1998).

Despite the perceived success of flagship developments in securing the revitalisation of downtowns, anecdotal evidence is beginning to suggest that such strategies are attracting little new inward investment or having any discernible impact on job creation. For example, although Pittsburgh is heralded in numerous reports as a success story of urban entrepreneurialism because of its vastly-improved image, revitalised city centre and restructured economic base, it nevertheless had the second-highest black poverty rate among the 20 largest metropolitan areas (36.2%) in 1990, and the sixth-highest male unemployment rate (12.1%) in 1993 (Leitner and Sheppard, 1998).

Empirical evidence to support "spill-over effects" is not very strong. Although, in successful cases, improved city image is reflected in an increase in the number of tourists and demand for tourism-related services, the strongly consumption-oriented nature of such strategies often makes it difficult for economic impacts to be felt beyond the service sectors which are immediately related to tourism. The newly-generated jobs are often not of the quality that diversify and modernise local economic structures. For example, according to a study assessing the impacts of entrepreneurial strategies in Birmingham, while such strategies succeeded in creating a limited number of jobs through its prestige development programme, these were primarily poorly-paid or part-time positions in service sector employment (Hall and Hubbard, 1998). Even the increase in the number of visitors would quickly fall back to the previous level after the novelty of the new investment is depreciated. This problem is particularly evident in the strategies of hosting major events that are held on a one-off basis rather than on a regular basis. In such cases, restructuring effects on the local economy as a whole would be rather limited.

Thus, it would be fair to say that the trickle-down effect theory appears to be based not so much on empirical facts as on the strong belief that everyone would benefit if a city economy was strengthened as a whole. However, so far, policy planners have not been particularly successful in translating short-term impacts of strategic approaches into long-term policy results that redress the long-standing urban issues, and it is increasingly becoming clear that the process of trickling-down is not as self-realising as many policy planners might wish. Conscious policy efforts would be vital to connect short-term gains to long-lasting economic restructuring.

One of the areas to be looked at appears to be the lack of attention to long-term policy programmes for building up local economic capacities, such as education and training, strengthening the technological levels of indigenous economic sectors, and investment in basic infrastructure. For example, the relative absence of additional regeneration strategies for urban regeneration was one of the issues raised by the House of Commons Employment Committee, United Kingdom, with regard to the London Docklands Development Corporation (LDDC). Although acknowledging its physical achievements, the committee thought "the LDDC should seek from the start to strike a reasonable balance between the physical development of the areas, and the social and other needs of those living there". The LDDC has paid scant attention to housing and social facilities (HCEC, 1988). Similar observation was made with regard to the Honeysuckle Development, Newcastle, New South Wales, Australia. Whereas the distribution of benefits resulting from the material reconstruction of Newcastle's inner area relies heavily on a trickle down mechanism, there was scant attention paid to the issue of adapting the local skills base and employment needs, resulting from the city's industrial legacy, to the anticipated employment generated in services and administration, festival shopping areas, entertainment and leisure complexes of the development (McGuirk, et al., 1998).

These are the fundamental preconditions for economic opportunities created by strategic projects to be fully exploited by local actors. Academic literature shows that an insufficient standard of local skills and quality of local products hinders the development of forward and backward linkages. The initial economic impacts triggered by the strategic projects can develop into wider economic effects of long-standing consequence only when necessary social and economic conditions are fulfilled. Too much emphasis on city promotional objectives might have caused the relative lack of policy planners' interest in integrating wider issues in overall urban regeneration policies.

When such a shift of policy planners' interest from long-term capacity-building programmes to short-term gains is accompanied by actual diversion of public resources to short-term promotional goals, as was illustrated in the case of Birmingham (see Box 2.4), the detrimental effects on the city's long-term competitiveness would not be negligible. Such a situation has often been caused by financial loss from the entrepreneurial projects. For example, Sheffield's 1991 Student Games, which burdened the local population with a large long-term debt repayment to be met from council taxes; Atlanta's Omni Centre, a mixed sports, office and hotel complex, similarly received massive state funding, but proved to be one of the biggest real estate disasters in history (Rutheiser, 1996). Many similar cases can be found in other countries. In fact, many of the image-enhancing schemes which have been promoted as profit-making have turned out to be loss-making (Hall and Hubbard, 1998). Such a situation is the risk accompanying property-led developments, which are inherently speculative due to the volatility of the property market. The question to be asked is whether it is a sound policy choice to take such a risk at the cost of severe fiscal constraints on long-term programmes to build up local economic capacities.

The short-termism at the expense of long-term capacity-building of local economies is a pitfall to be avoided by policy planners. Competitive local economies can only be achieved by nurturing fundamental strength over the long-term; attractive physical environments created by prestigious developments can contribute to it, but as Turok (1992) articulates, a "one-club" approach cannot achieve the goal.

Another approach is related to a more fundamental reflection in strategy planning. Even if a city cannot attract internationally-mobile investment in the short term, it is often the case that it still possesses indigenous sectors with a competitive edge in certain fields, which can grow and expand. However, in some examples, indigenous sectors have not been paid sufficient policy attention and given adequate resources in a situation where too much preoccupation with city-promotional objectives, prompted by the urgency and sheer magnitude of rapid industrial decline, eclipsed other "sober" approaches. Policy planners' urge to find expedient solutions is understandable, but the neglect of local assets would cost the city dear in the long term.

Under the circumstance that internationally-mobile capital's interest is limited to a small number of cities, new growth momentum cannot easily be grafted from outside onto a city. In the worst cases, it simply causes various types of dislocation within the functional region where a city is located and produces no visible impact on the overall regional economy. For a city without much of a profile on the global market, economic success by the indigenous sectors is an important step to achieve a wider recognition as a destination of business location. Some empirical studies suggest that seminal agglomeration

> ### Box 2.4. **Budget diversion: Birmingham's case**
>
> Pro-growth strategy (and, in particular, its investment in prestige projects) has brought numerous benefits to Birmingham, including the creation of a new and dynamic image, the physical transformation of the city centre, the generation of a significant number of new jobs, and the attraction of much-needed private sector investment into the city.
>
> However, it is also argued that the city council's strategy has resulted in a diversion of scarce city council resources away from essential services such as education and housing – particularly affecting the city's most disadvantaged communities – and relatively few economic benefits for disadvantaged residents and neighbourhoods.
>
> It was estimated that Birmingham lost GBP 599 million in central government rate support grants between 1981 and 1990. Under such circumstances, where central government cuts support for local authority expenditure considerably, Birmingham City Council's significant financial investment in prestige developments resulted in significant diversion of public resources away from "basic" services which the city's disadvantaged groups are particularly dependent upon. For example, the two prestige developments, the International Convention Centre (ICC) and National Indoor Arena (NIA), accounted for 18% of total Birmingham City Council capital spending (amounting to 228 million) over the period 1986/87-1991/92.
>
> It was the city's education revenue budget which was the most adversely affected by the cost of city promotional activities and the operational losses of the ICC and NIA. Between 1991/92 and 1995/96 the ICC and NIA accrued an accumulated operational deficit of GBP 146 million, a deficit which was exacerbated by large expenditure on prestigious arts events, the Birmingham Super Prix and the bid for the 1992 Olympics.
>
> The effect of this revenue expenditure meant that between 1988 and 1993 the city council's revenue expenditure on education was consistently lower than that recommended by central government, and in 1990/91 the city council's GBP 46 million revenue underspent on education accounted for nearly half of the national education budget underspent. The council's capital spending on the education service also fell by 60% during the construction of the prestige projects.
>
> Spending on housing was also significantly affected by such strategies. Over the period 1986/87-1991/92 the city council spent GBP 123 million less on housing than the average performance of local authorities in England. This spending profile occurred despite an outstanding repairs bill for council housing of GBP 1.3 billion and the existence of 81 251 homes in the city which were unfit for human habitation.
>
> Source: Loftman, P. and B. Nevin (1996), "Going for Growth: Prestige Projects in Three British Cities", *Urban Studies*, Vol. 33, pp. 991-1019.

of local entrepreneurs plays a crucial role in initiating a self-reinforcing process of agglomeration, which is characteristic of many spontaneous growth points (Torisu, 1986). The strengthening of indigenous sectors is also important, as was already discussed, to fully assimilate the economic impacts brought about by the inward investment, if it does occur, and spread them among the local economies. Exogenous and indigenous sectors are not a choice of "either/or", but need to be fully integrated into long-term strategies so that a self-reinforcing process, where indigenous sectors contribute to strengthening the city's profile on the market and exogenous sectors, in return, contribute to an increase in the competitiveness of the indigenous sectors, occurs.

2.4. Competition and co-operation

There is also the pitfall of "blind faith" in market forces that assumes that once property is available for development, financial and business services will take advantage of the opportunity. As McGuirk, et al. (1998) warn, the prospects for this are not overly hopeful. Under the current circumstances, where inter-city competition to attract inward investment has become sharper as more and more cities are joining in the race to offer more and more inducements for inward investment, offering "more of the same" and betting enormous amounts in order to place a city onto the global market could sometimes be a misguided strategy. The attractiveness of economic enticements to outside investors is considerably reduced by the availability of similar incentives at numerous other locations, nationally and internationally. Such a situation, together with standardised landscapes of standardised land-use mixes produced by many flagship developments, would cancel out the benefits of place marketing based on these developments.

Furthermore, in such a race offering more of the same, net benefits may diminish not only for individual cities but for the broader system as a whole. Cities engaged in such strategies increasingly find themselves locked into a buyers' market, in which firms are able to play one city off against another and demand ever more generous subsidies. It is widely acknowledged that this was the cause of extreme cases of bidding wars among US cities. For example, in 1994, the city of Amarillo, Texas, sent 1 300 US companies a check for USD 8 million, to be redeemed if the company committed to creating at least 700 new jobs in Amarillo. In the same year, St Louis, Missouri, sought to attract a professional American football team at an estimated cost of USD 720 million to state and local taxpayers (Leitner and Sheppard, 1998). A recent comparative study of the incentives offered by US cities also showed that the costs associated with attracting investors may outweigh the benefits for economically disadvantaged cities by demonstrating that cities with high levels of unemployment tendentially offer greater incentives to potential investors, but, despite this, do not increase their overall attractiveness for investment relative to cities with low unemployment (Fisher and Peters, 1996). In this way, bidding wars can reinforce a general trend to divert public resources for short-term gains at the expense of longer-term investments in the city's economic capacity-building.

The creation of a buyers' market can have deleterious effects on a region as a whole, because even when such a mix of enticements can attract inward investment, it was pointed out, the attraction of firms to the newly-renovated city centres was achieved often by short-distance transfers within the same labour-market areas without producing overall gains in employment on a city-wide basis. For example, in Glasgow, it was reported that the largest amounts of new floor space have been taken up by existing firms and government departments, and little success was achieved in attracting high-level office functions and corporate headquarters (Turok, 1992). Even in cases where long-distance relocations occurred, it was often the case that such relocations originated from more disadvantaged areas. For example, it was found that in the United Kingdom 60% of long-distance transfers to the Enterprise Zones actually originated from areas with average or above-average unemployment rates (Turok, 1992). Even if such an initial concentration of firms through intra-regional relocation is justified on the grounds of the necessity to form a critical mass, as in the case of spill-over effects, it must be shown that wider areas would eventually benefit from the process. However, as Turok (1992) points out, policy approaches based on a limited geographical scope make it difficult to pursue co-ordinated metropolitan-area-wide or region-wide development, which clearly points to the need for policy co-ordination and co-operation on a wider geographic scale. Such a policy approach is already happening, and should be further promoted (see Box 2.5).

Place competition on a narrowly defined geographical scope does not necessarily produce overall gains, and often results in competition for the relocation of firms within the same city-region. This pitfall of place-based strategies would be overcome by creating a co-operative framework of cities that belong to the same functional economic area. It also enables public bodies to tackle strategic issues beyond municipal borders. Such a collective approach necessitates better co-ordination of the public bodies involved, both vertically and horizontally, which is a recurring theme in metropolitan governance. Much progress is being made in this field, and there is still much scope for policy innovation.

Conclusions: pitfalls in the entrepreneurial approach

Entrepreneurial approaches to urban regeneration opened up a new dimension in urban policy planning by making important contributions to it. Much policy innovation has been achieved by applying corporate strategic

Box 2.5. **The Northern Way**

The Northern Way in the United Kingdom is an example of an approach to enhance attractiveness that operates at the city-regional level. It has been instrumental in identifying joint priorities across the north of England, common strengths and weaknesses of northern regions and areas of collaboration that can add value to the activities being undertaken in each region individually. The strategic direction is developed by the Northern Way Steering Group, and consists of long-term strategies combining economic, environmental and social objectives in the north of England, in collaboration with Government and regional stakeholders. Recently the Steering Group published a Growth Strategy which seeks to identify potential areas of co-operation between the three Regional Development Agencies, the local authorities, the Regional Assemblies (Yorkshire Forward, One NorthEast and the Northwest Regional Development Agency), public-private partnerships, and Learning and Skills Councils, among others.

Through a wide range of priorities and projects the Northern Way aims to link city competitiveness and attractiveness with policies to promote social inclusion. Some of its main priorities are to: increase employment, strengthen the knowledge base, promote entrepreneurship, capture a larger share of global trade through clusters, ensure that the workforce is sufficiently skilled to meet employer needs, improve access to airports and sea ports, improve the transit system, create sustainable communities and market the north to the rest of world.

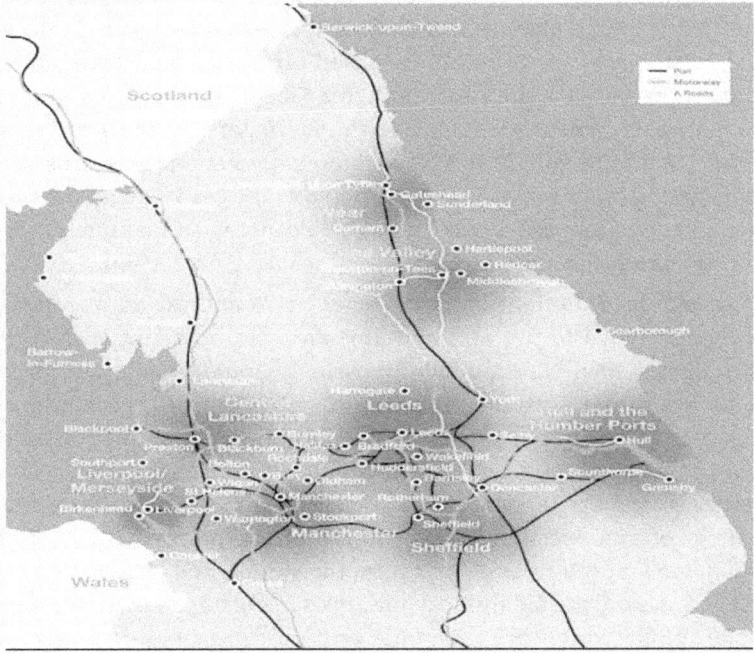

Source: : The Northern Way, *www.thenorthernway.co.uk/*.

planning methodology to public policy planning and by identifying and exploiting the potential of policy tools that were not originally included in the portfolio of urban policy planning. Resources have been strategically allocated for spatial development to maximise the positive effects of city promotion and branding. Strategic alliances were formed between the public and private sectors, and often business played a key role in the process.

In the era of globally-integrated economies and markets and the ever-intensifying inter-city, inter-regional competition for inward investment and mobile talent, entrepreneurialism has, over the past decades, become an essential element in urban spatial development policy, and it will continue to be so in future. It is now widely acknowledged that the extent to which a city can achieve this paradigm shift will determine its competitiveness in the global market.

However, policy experience over the past decades in OECD countries has also shown that there are certain pitfalls in this approach to be avoided in order to ensure truly fruitful outcomes in the long run. First, the serial reproduction of a handful of successful cases is leading to the loss of local distinctiveness and character of our built-environment. It is also creating a similar set of policy components in urban regeneration across the globe no matter what the local conditions and historical context. Attracting investment and talent increasingly requires distinguishing the social, physical and cultural character of a place as location; and place marketing originally aimed to differentiate one city from others based on its unique assets and built-environment. However, the new marketed "local" identity has often been indistinguishable from a mass of other similar waterfront/leisure places, and offers little that is unique to the place in an era when place is considered to have a resurging importance. This is particularly the case when it necessitates sacrificing the uniqueness of what the local economy and culture could offer in order to reproduce a post-modern "blandscape" (Short, 1989).

Flagship developments and other entrepreneurial approaches were originally conceived to put a "signature" on a city to distinguish it on the global market, which is becoming increasingly homogeneous. However, the ironic situation that entrepreneurial approaches are strengthening, rather than counter-acting, the homogenising effects of globalisation is significantly undermining the effectiveness of place marketing strategies, which often necessitate a considerable amount of public investment. It also casts doubt on the strategy of attempting redevelopment in a manner that is already being done, and done more successfully, at other locations, and clearly points to the importance of more genuinely local initiatives to nurture local identities based on social, environmental, economic and cultural resources that a city possesses as its unique assets.

More fundamentally, nurturing local identities attractive to investors and entrepreneurs require long-term policy efforts to build up indigenous assets such as an entrepreneurial business climate and a high level of education and skill bases. This argument leads to the second pitfall of urban entrepreneurialism, short-termism, that is to say, the pursuit of short-term gains by simply attracting external elements at the expense of long-term approaches to build up the economic fundamentals in the city by the improvement of education, job-training and housing and the enhancement of indigenous economic sectors' technological base.

Many local governments are allocating increasingly high amounts of their budgets to city promotion strategies (Savitch and Kantor, 1995) in manifestation of the entrepreneurial approach. However, excessive occupation with the narrow aspects of city attractiveness, particularly its physical attractiveness as a post-industrial city represented by flagship city centre developments, sometimes obscured the importance of building up the capacities of local economies in the long term. When the operational loss of such flagship developments aggravate the fiscal constraints on policy programmes for education, job-training and technological development of local firms, the detrimental effects on the local economy will perpetuate. Such a situation is totally contrary to what urban economic regeneration objectives envisaged in the first place.

The neglect of long-term policy objectives could lead to the dualism of image and reality, to which much academic criticism of place promotion has been directed. In such a situation, city promotion strategies are labelled a "carnival mask" that creates the impression of regeneration and vibrancy within cities, but, in reality, do nothing to address the underlying problems that necessitated regeneration programmes in the first place (Harvey, 1988). Such a pitfall of short-termism should be avoided by the long term perspectives that policy planners must always keep in mind in policy planning.

The third point is that the long-term viability and effectiveness of strategic approaches rests on the extent to which the local residents share such strategic objectives with policy planners. However, the excessive emphasis on attracting external elements inherent in place promotion sometimes alienates local residents. The image propagated by place promotion strategies often envisages wealthy urban professionals as the targeted audience. The new land use to be realised by flagship development projects is often planned so that it only appeals to the tastes and demands of this group of people. In such a situation, the residents find it difficult to establish a connection between such strategic approaches and their quality of life.

In order to acquire residents' support, which is essential for the sustainable implementation of strategic programmes, it is crucial, first of all, to make it clear to residents that such strategies are built on the premise that the enhancement of the quality of residents' lives forms the core of city attractiveness. Secondly, the local residents' capacity for strategic thinking should be enhanced. They should be allowed a chance to think strategically about the economic issues that their city faces. To build such capacity in residents, learning experience is essential. Such experience should be gained in an inclusive and open process in strategy planning with a wide range of participants. An institutional framework in which the interests of the community are truly represented, is essential to support such a process. The enhancement of communication skills of public officials to interact with a wide spectrum of the local constituency is also crucial to initiate and facilitate the process.

ISBN 978-92-64-02240-9
OECD Territorial Review
Competitive Cities
A New Entrepreneurial Paradigm in Spatial Develompent
© OECD 2007

Chapter 3

A Market-oriented Approach in Building and Housing Policies

> This chapter reviews market-oriented approaches in building and housing policies, which have recently been the prominent trend. It analyses the regulatory reforms that change building regulations and zoning controls to be performance-based, rather than specification-based as they have traditionally been, in order to encourage private innovations, as well as information instruments and privatisation of social housing. Furthermore, the chapter analyses how market-oriented approaches could achieve public goals more effectively, not just by following market forces but by positively interacting with them.

Introduction

In recent decades one of the most important directions in building and housing policy has been market orientation. Since buildings are primarily supplied and allocated in the building market, one of the greatest concerns in building policy has been market functionality. As for housing provision, in the 1980s and 1990s, many governments retreated from ambitious public housing programmes that demanded heavy, unsustainable subsidies and have increasingly opted for programmes relying on the market function, rather than direct production, mainly against the background of pressure to reduce public expenditure.

While this trend towards a market-oriented approach in building and housing policy manifests itself as various policy measures, such as privatisation, regulatory reform and promotion of information instruments, the trend in general can be described as a move away from the role of government as direct producer or regulator, to a new role as enabler, facilitating and encouraging building and housing activities by the private sector through market mechanisms to achieve policy objectives, coupled with reduced levels of government support and greater independence of the building and housing sector.

While these measures have achieved initial policy objectives (or at least are intended to achieve such objectives), in some cases, unintended consequences have emerged, which cannot easily be addressed by past or current market-oriented approaches; in other cases, these measures could not work as effectively as expected. The aim of this chapter is to clarify how the policy approach in the field of building and housing has changed – reflecting the market-oriented trend – and is now changing, in the new circumstances, towards a more desirable policy direction, focusing on three policy measures: 1) regulatory reform to enhance the flexibility of building regulations and planning systems; 2) promotion of information instruments to vitalise the housing market; and 3) privatisation and decentralisation in social housing policy.

1. Policy reviews

1.1. Regulatory reform to enhance the flexibility of regulations

In many countries, various types of regulations have been designed and implemented to reduce the causes of inefficient functioning of markets, such as externality and asymmetric information, which could cause market failure. For instance, since building purchasers cannot easily examine building quality (asymmetric information), "building regulations" are required to protect the public from defective buildings. As another example, since the regulation-free land market could allow land use incompatible with the use of neighbouring properties (negative externality), "zoning regulations" are necessary to prevent such land use. On the other hand, such government intervention could also cause inefficiency in market functioning. For instance, excessive or unnecessary regulations could be the cause of market inefficiency by impeding market players from operating flexibly and competitively. It is becoming one of the primary challenges for policymakers to reduce these negative effects of government intervention in the market and to promote private sector innovation and creativity. Against this backdrop, many countries are trying to enhance the flexibility of these regulations.

Recent trends in regulatory reform aimed at enhancing the efficiency of the market by means of two types of regulatory instruments – building regulation and planning systems (zoning regulation) – are examined in this section. First, regulatory reform aimed at promoting renovation and conversion of existing buildings by improving the flexibility of building regulations is examined. Inflexible building regulations often impede renovation and conversion of existing buildings, which has a negative impact on the sustainability of building stock. In many countries more flexible regulations which promote such renovation and conversion through market mechanisms have been designed and implemented. Secondly, regulatory reform contributing to mitigating the competing pressures of complex issues, such as housing affordability and environmental concerns, through the market system by increasing the flexibility of zoning regulation is reviewed. While zoning regulations have been implemented to separate incompatible land uses and thereby reduce negative externality in the land market, they could impede flexible land use, which might lead to various problems such as housing affordability. Some countries have been tackling this issue by enhancing the flexibility of zoning regulation.

1.1.1. Regulatory reform in building regulations

The traditional form of building regulations was to specify requirements in prescriptive terms. However, if building regulation is based on prescriptive codes not allowing for flexibility in design, there would be less possibility of reducing the renovation costs by innovative use of materials, forms of structure or design. Therefore, some countries are now applying special standards for renovation.

While prescriptive codes describe an acceptable solution, performance-based codes describe the required performance. For instance, as for fire safety, a prescriptive code would specify what materials the structural frame of buildings should or should not be made of; whereas performance-based codes might state that the building structure should be able to withstand a fire long enough for the occupants to escape safely, but would not prescribe what materials must or must not be used.

As Foliente (2000) points out, prescriptive codes have three problems: they serve as a barrier to innovation, make it difficult to cost-optimise building construction, and impede international trade in building products by making it difficult to establish equivalence between codes adopted in different countries/regions. Performance-based codes are expected to free building regulatory systems from such limitations. The trend towards performance-based codes coincided with the trend in many countries to reduce the regulatory burden of building codes, make regulations clearer and reducing the overall cost impact on regulators (IRCC, 2000). As a result, following early adoption in the United Kingdom and New Zealand, pressures for changes in building codes led many countries to introduce performance-based codes since the late 1990s (Table 3.1).

Table 3.1. **Development of performance-based building codes in OECD countries**

Year	Country	
1985	United Kingdom*	The Building Regulations were extensively revised in 1985 by using functional or performance wording instead of prescriptive requirements.
1993	New Zealand	The 1992 version of the New Zealand Building Code was promulgated as a performance-based document and was enforced on 1 January 1993.
1997/98	Australia	The Australian Building Codes Board released the performance-based Building Code of Australia (BCA) in October 1996, which was adopted by most of the States and Territories in 1997, and the remainder in 1998.
1998	Japan	The Building Standards Law was amended in 1998 and the performance-based standards were enforced in June 2000.
2000	US	The International Code Council (ICC) released a performance-based model code "Performance Code for Buildings and Facilities (ICCPC)" in 2000. The adoption of codes is a state or local decision. A move to allow the ICCPC as a compliance option has been observed.
2003	Canada	The objective-based model national building, fire and plumbing codes are scheduled to be published by the Canadian Commission on Building and Fire Codes (CCBFC) in 2005. The adoption of codes is the responsibility of provincial or territorial authorities having jurisdiction.

* England and Wales.
Source: IRCC homepage: *www.ircc.gov.au/*; Gann, David M., Yusi Wang and Richard Hawkins (1998), "Do Regulations Encourage Innovation?: The Case of Energy Efficiency in Housing", *Building Research and Information*, Vol. 26, No. 4, pp. 280-296; Meacham, Brian J. (1998), *The Evolution of Performance-Based Codes and Fire Safety Design Methods*, NIST (National Institute of Standards and Technology, US Department of Commerce), Gaithersburg; Duncan, John (2005), "Performance-Based Building: Lessons from Implementation in New Zealand", *Building Research and Information*, Vol. 33, No. 2, March-April, pp. 120-127; ICC homepage: *www.iccsafe.org/cs/resources/performance.html*; National Resource Council Canada homepage: *www.nationalcodes.ca/ncd_home_e.shtml*.

Since performance-based codes allow innovative use of materials, forms of construction and design, as well as designs tailored to the targeted existing building, they are expected to promote sustainable use of building stock through market mechanisms by cost-optimising renovation and conversion.

However, experience in countries which were early in adopting performance-based codes suggests that careful implementation is required to capture these advantages. For instance, by examining the performance-based regulation of energy efficiency in the United Kingdom, Gann, et al. (1998) point out that the risk-averse characteristic of the construction sector leads to a conservative approach with respect to new technologies. As a result, the construction sector is usually wary of and resistant to innovation. Even if innovative and flexible use of materials and forms of construction or design are enabled by performance-based standards, the construction industry prefers to stick to the "deemed to satisfy" route, which is based on traditional or existing technologies.

Such a conservative characteristic of the construction industry increases the significance of downstream users in promoting innovation. The Civil Engineering Research Foundation conference held in the United States in 2000 identified creation of "market pull", by provision of reliable information to potential users about the expected benefits of innovation, as a key strategy to put innovation into practice for a sustainable future construction sector (Duncan, 2005). Moreover, the multiple objectives and compliance mechanisms of performance-based codes create complexity which is unlikely to stimulate change. Therefore, Gann, et al. (1998) point out that clarity and simplicity are needed in the regulatory process to enable the up-take of good practice and encourage innovation.

Apart from the United Kingdom, New Zealand is one of the earliest adopters of a performance building code. However, the introduction of the new code in 1992 was not accompanied by extensive industry education. As a result, two enquires commissioned in 2002 and 2003 concluded that there had been systematic failure in the industry. There was criticism of the extent of education and training in the sector, and of the extent of technical innovation without the benefit of experience and understanding, and concern expressed about the asymmetry of information between the industry and its clients (Duncan, 2005). Industry participants might follow the "deemed to satisfy" route, even if it was not necessarily the best long-term result for the building owner who was recognised probably not to have the expertise to know the alternatives available.

Therefore, in order to make the performance-based codes work more effectively in the building market and thereby promote cost-optimised renovation and conversion, policy makers should introduce simplified performance-based codes accompanied by provision of sufficient reliable information to potential users of the code as well as well-focused training programmes for all involved in the design and construction process. In other word, consideration for the adaptability of the market is a key for successful introduction of these innovative regulations.

1.1.2. Regulatory reform in planning systems

The housing affordability problem, indicating a situation where housing prices rise more sharply than the increase in household income, is aggravated by the price inelasticity of housing supply, to which many factors are said to contribute. One such factor is the negative effects of certain types of government intervention, particularly regulations that limit land supply and impose additional costs on residential development. Hence, attempts are being made in member countries to minimise such negative effects of governmental intervention. This part examines performance-based zoning systems, which have the potential to minimise such negative effects by enhancing the flexibility of planning systems.

When introduced in the early 1900s in several countries such as the United States, zoning was designed to prevent the harm that could result from land use that conflicts with the use of neighbouring properties. In order to prevent such harm, traditional zoning ordinances separate land use in a hierarchy based on land use type. They divide communities into specific "zones" that permit only "compatible" land use, which often results in the segregation of use, such as commercial, industrial, single-family residential, and multi-family residential usages.

Although traditional zoning ordinances have had significant impacts in preventing such harm, they are not designed to deal with the complexities of a changing, dynamic world. They are incapable of resolving the competing pressures of complex issues such as environmental concerns, decaying infrastructure, suburban sprawl, and shortage of affordable housing (Eggers, 1990). As a result, traditional zoning usually allows a proliferation of zoning districts, and is administered as an *ad hoc* reaction to land development proposals. The result is changes to zoned areas over time by variances, conditional uses, special use permits, etc., which makes zoning a continuing process of *ad hoc* administrative decisions (Baker, *et al.*, 2004).

In practice, a continual procession of changes and amendments in the zoning codes provides no certainty to neighbourhood residents who often find their neighbourhoods subject to re-zoning. The process often leads to unfairness, as exceptions to the rigid regulations of zoning are tossed out in an unsystematic, and, at times, in a purely political fashion (Eggers, 1990). In order to overcome such problems and the politicisation generated by traditional zoning, it is necessary to, for instance: 1) make the approval criteria explicit and subject to measurable standards; 2) make the decisions by authorities more predictable, less arbitrary and less subjective; and 3) replace negotiations with administrative decision making. In order to achieve such outcomes, several countries have attempted to introduce "performance-based planning".

Performance-based planning regulates land use based not on the proposed use, location and dimensions of the development, but on the basis of the actual impacts it will have on the neighbouring residents and businesses. It allows any land use to locate adjacent to any other use, provided it satisfies pre-determined performance standards (Alexander, et al., 2002). The concept of "performance zoning system" was first developed by Lane Kendig in 1973 when he was Director of Community Planning for Bucks County, Pennsylvania. According to Freiden, et al. (1997), Kendig explains that "performance zoning does not organise uses into a hierarchy which is then used to protect 'higher' uses from 'lower' ones. Rather, it imposes minimum levels of performance by setting standards that must be met by each land use".

According to Eggers (1990), the city of Fort Collins, Colorado was first to introduce a system mostly based on the concept developed by Kendig. The city was located in one of the most rapidly growing areas in the United States, and wanted a system that was responsive to market forces on one hand, and, on the other, offered some quality control over what was going to happen on a site. In 1981, the city of Fort Collins dropped traditional zoning and replaced it with the Land Development Guidance System (LDGS), which provided performance criteria for planned unit developments (PUDs). The LDGS is based on the belief that the free market should dictate the locations and types of land use in the community (CMHC, 2000). A point system is used to determine the value of each development proposal (see Box 3.1).

Since local authorities had relatively little discretion over the content of the proposed development once the formula was established in the zoning code and evaluation process, the system streamlined the development application and approval process. As a result, the average time required for the application/review process was decreased from 7-9 months to 7-14 weeks (Eggers, 1990). However, the points-based system in Fort Collins was revised in 1997 because of political challenges and a growing desire for a planning system with more predictable outcomes (Tomalty, et al., 2000). According to Baker, et al. (2004), among the eight US local governments which introduced performance-based planning systems since the 1970s, only one (Breckenridge, Colorado) remained committed to the original performance-based approach. Two dropped the performance-based approach and the other five revised the system. According to an overview of performance-based planning commissioned by the town of Breckenridge, the two primary reasons for this

> **Box 3.1. Point system for evaluating development proposals, Fort Collins, United States**
>
> In the Land Development Guidance System (LDGS), development plans were evaluated based on the number of "points" they accumulated; the overall score for the proposed project was determined by multipliers attached to the performance and impact criteria in LDGS, and so long as the development plan achieved an established minimum number of points, it was approved by local planners. Each residential proposal must achieve at least the minimum percentage points required for the proposed density (*e.g.*, 100 or more percentage points are required for a proposal with 10 or more dwellings units per acre). The proposed density is refused if the minimum score is not reached. The percentage points could be earned, by, for instance, containing affordable housing or reducing non-renewable energy usage.
>
> Source: CMHC (Canada Mortgage and Housing Corporation) (2000), *Research Report: International Experiences with Performance-Based Planning*, Housing Affordability and Finance Series, CMHC.

shift away from performance-based planning were the lack of land-use guidelines resulting in community uncertainty, and difficulties in explaining and applying complex performance standards.

The trade-off between predictability and flexibility makes it difficult to introduce "pure" performance-based systems. While the developers are allowed a great deal of flexibility under performance-based land-use regulations in determining the use of land, at times they find the process unpredictable, and not guided by clear and specific rules and procedures (Eggers, 1990). Performance-based planning faces significant challenges in promoting flexibility when many stakeholders (including developers and the community) call for predictability. In this regard, the practice in Australia offering a choice to developers between a conventional solution and a performance-based solution is effective in improving both the predictability and flexibility of planning systems by making the two solutions complement each other (see Box 3.2).

1.1.3. *Toward effective regulatory reform to enhance the flexibility of regulations*

As seen above, many OECD countries are trying to improve the flexibility of building and zoning regulations towards a market-oriented approach. While regulations could reduce the causes of inefficient functioning of markets, they could also cause market inefficiency by impeding market players from operating flexibly and competitively. To reduce the negative

> **Box 3.2. Performance-based planning system, Australia**
>
> In Australia a property boom coincided with very high levels of immigration in the late 1980s, causing skyrocketing housing prices in metropolitan areas. To address housing affordability by promoting higher density residential development in urban areas, the federal government proposed a national framework of performance-based planning principles and procedures for high-quality residential development. Based on this idea, various versions of the Australian Model Code for Residential Development (AMCORD) promoted the concept of performance-based planning. Every state/territory government in Australia has now adopted its own AMCORD-based model code. AMCORD is centred on objectives and desired outcomes (performance), instead of the specification of prescriptive standards. Developers can take advantage of the flexibility of the performance criteria without being held back by restrictive regulations. As an alternative, they can also choose certainty by basing design on a series of acceptable solutions, i.e., examples of how to achieve the desired result. It is possible to design depending on either performance criteria or on acceptable solutions.
>
> Source: CMHC (Canada Mortgage and Housing Corporation) (2000), *Research Report: International Experiences with Performance-Based Planning*, Housing Affordability and Finance Series, CMHC.

effects of government intervention in the building and housing market and pursue a market-oriented approach, enhancing the flexibility of those regulations by, for example, introducing performance-based regulations is essential. Regulations should not impede private-sector innovation and creativity while attempting to achieve initial objectives, such as addressing obstacles hindering efficient functioning of the market.

On the other hand, experience in some countries which were early in adopting innovative regulations suggests that careful implementation is required to make such regulations work effectively in the market. Implementation of innovative regulatory reform, such as introduction of performance-based regulations, cannot be done simply by imposing them on the market. Successful introduction of such regulatory reform must be accompanied by consideration of its adaptability to the market. Governments should play a key role in enhancing such adaptability by, for instance, providing sufficient information on expected outcomes from the regulatory reform to market players, including downstream users, and offering necessary options to address challenges such as the trade-off between flexibility and predictability.

1.2. Promotion of information instruments to vitalise the housing market

One of the key factors to enable the market to work efficiently is information. The basic requirement for the efficient functioning of markets is the provision of sufficient information for market players on both the supply and demand sides. For instance, if information is unevenly distributed between demanders and suppliers – *i.e.*, there is asymmetric information – adverse selection may occur, which will lead to impeding active transactions by market players.[1] To address asymmetric information and vitalise the housing market, information instruments play a key role. This section focuses on information instruments aimed at addressing information failure in the housing market. First, information tools to vitalise the housing resale market, which contribute to sustainable use of building stock, are examined. Second, information systems which provide information related to rental housing for the elderly and thereby enhance housing availability for the elderly are reviewed.

1.2.1. Information tools to vitalise the housing resale market

In the housing market, there is a lack of information on the buyers' side which hinders the efficient functioning of the market. Due to the high capital cost of buildings, many buyers, especially individual consumers, have few opportunities for "learning by buying". Consequently, prospective buyers tend to lack information on the quality of the buildings they are going to buy. Moreover, those who are in the market for existing buildings have more difficulty collecting information on housing quality than those who are in the new building market. This is because the quality of existing housing is affected not only by their design but also by how they have been used and maintained, and also because it is usually more difficult to evaluate their performance. As the result of such lack of information, buyers may overweight the probability of the risk of quality inferiority, which will prevent them from entering the housing resale market.

In some OECD countries, policy makers are increasingly concerned with housing resale market issues as a factor that affects the sustainable use of building stock. Vitalising the housing resale market by improving market efficiency would contribute to minimising the mismatch between supply and demand in the housing resale market and help housing stock meet potential owners' space demands for longer periods of time. Therefore, vitalising the housing resale market is seen as an important factor for the sustainable use of building stock.

For instance, in Japan, information failure significantly impedes the growth of the housing resale market. According to a public opinion poll conducted by the Cabinet Office in November 2004, the percentage of those preferring newly constructed housing amounted to 82.2%. As for the reasons these people preferred new construction, 41.9% pointed out the freedom to choose planning and design they prefer, 34.4% pointed out the good feeling of owning something totally new, and 10.6% responded that they were afraid of defects related to seismic safety, thermal insulation, etc. Figure 3.1 shows the results of a questionnaire survey of home buyers who bought new and existing housing over a two-year period in Japan. Out of 700 respondents, 62% answered that warranty for possible defects in structural parts of housing and other measures to cope with housing defects should be implemented to help develop the resale market in Japan. In addition, 52% responded that information about maintenance and renovation work that has been conducted in the past should be provided to prospective buyers. These results suggest that buyers of existing buildings are not provided with sufficient information regarding the quality of the housing they are seeking to buy, nor on the quality of its maintenance. In addition to the general preference for newly produced goods, fear of hidden defects impedes the expansion of the market. The limited size of the market constricts the scope of choice, which leads to further shrinkage of the market. This is the vicious circle of the housing resale market in Japan.

Figure 3.1. **Requirements for developing the housing resale market in Japan**

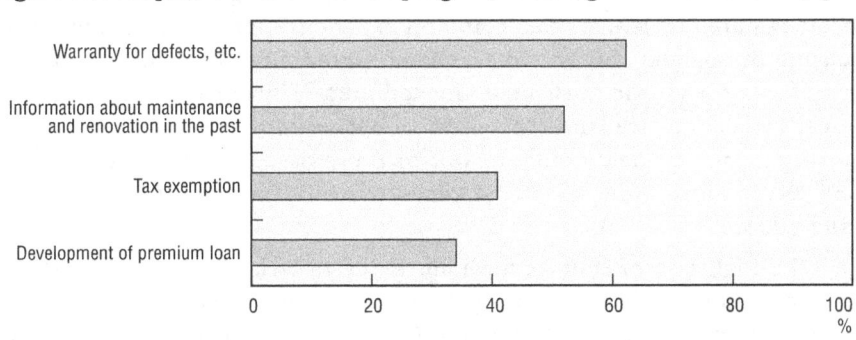

Source: Japan Real Estate Trade Association (2002), Survey on Consumers' Behaviour related to Real Estates Trade, on-line document.

Many OECD countries have a larger housing resale market compared to Japan (Table 3.2). However, countries with a vital resale market, such as the United Kingdom, also suffer from various problems due to information failure in the resale market. In the case of Scotland, there is no obligation for a house seller to disclose any known defects of the property they are selling. The only warranty that a seller is bound to give is that they have a good title that can be passed on to the buyer. Since buyers have to conduct surveys in order to check

Table 3.2. **Size of the resale market compared to owner-occupied housing in selected OECD countries**

Unit: 1 000	Owner-occupied housing (a)	Number of resales (b)	b/a (%)
United Kingdom	14 916	1 586	10.63
United States	72 265	5 296	7.33
Denmark	1 285	91	7.08
France	15 714	775	4.93
Japan	26 468	157	0.59

Source: United Kingdom a: (England and Wales) Census (2001), b: (England and Wales) dated 2002 on ODPM website; United States a: American Housing Survey (2001), b: Statistical Abstract of the United States (2001); Denmark a: Statistics Denmark (2003), b: Sales of Real Estate (2001), Statistics Denmark; France a: Enquête Nationale Logement (2003/2004), b: Annuaire Statistique de la France (2000); Japan: 1998 Housing and Land Survey of Japan (a: 1998, b: 1997).

the condition of housing before bidding, almost a third of house purchasers commission more than one survey or valuation report. As a result, fear of forfeiting the cost of conducting surveys has reinforced the tendency of prospective purchasers to rely on the cheapest survey available – the valuation report which lenders require as part of the mortgage offer. Since such a report is not a comprehensive survey and may not fully reflect the actual condition of the property, 27% of house purchasers in Scotland had incurred unexpected repairs in the first year after purchase (Scottish Executive, 2002).

Facing unexpected repairs as a result of relying on the low-cost valuation report required by lenders is a common experience for purchasers of resale housing throughout the United Kingdom. According to research by a major firm of estate agents in the United Kingdom, 18% of buyers who relied on their lender's valuation faced unexpected repair bills within the first four months of moving into their new home. In 48% of these cases the bill amounted to GBP 500 or more, and in 17% of cases the bill exceeded GBP 1 000 (UK ODPM, 2004b).

The high rate of transaction failure due to lack of information at the agreement stage is also a serious problem in the United Kingdom. According to research conducted in 1998 by the UK government (DETR, 1998), 28% of accepted sales offers failed to proceed to completion. Forty-three percent of these failed transactions (i.e., 12% of all transactions) are due to condition-related problems being brought to light in either the buyer's survey or the lender's valuation inspection. The cost of failed transactions, such as conveyancing costs, mortgage valuation and survey fees, could be high. A typical failed transaction cost was found to be about GBP 900 (GBP 680 for buyers and GBP 226 for sellers). The research estimated that the total cost of transaction failure to consumers is at least GBP 350 million a year (UK ODPM, 2004c). Thus, there is room for improvement regarding information failure in the housing resale market both in countries with small and large resale markets.

1.2.1.1. Necessity to promote information disclosure schemes based on "caveat vendor". In order to address information failure and vitalise the resale market, the Japanese government expanded the Housing Performance Indication Scheme (HPIS) based on the Housing Quality Assurance Law and applied it to existing housing from 2002.[2] HPIS for existing housing is a comprehensive labelling system of housing performance, such as accessibility for the elderly, seismic safety, etc. Moreover, in order to cope with consumers' concerns regarding the quality of housing for resale, a quality assurance scheme for existing housing was introduced in 2001 by the Organization for Housing Warranty (OHW). The government provided financial support in order to reduce the assurance fee. The scheme provides quality assurance for a period of five years for housing that both meets certain requirements and passes the inspection organised by OHW.

However, these voluntary indication and assurance schemes have not been widely used by consumers. At the end of November 2004, 52 designated evaluation bodies were undertaking evaluation of HPIS for existing housing. While the number of evaluated units amounted to almost 400 thousand in the case of new construction as of the end of October 2004, in the case of existing housing, it amounted to only 357. At the end of November 2004, the number of housing units utilising the assurance scheme amounted to only 70. According to research conducted by OHW, 65% of the cases using the scheme were initiated by the seller and most of them were attempts to dispose of properties they failed to sell after new construction.

One reason why such indication and assurance schemes for existing housing are under-utilised is that both sellers and buyers of existing housing are usually reluctant to pay for such schemes. The seller usually expects to exploit their information advantage over the buyers and is afraid of forfeiting the expense for inspection in case the property fails to sell. Buyers are also reluctant to pay for detailed inspections. According to Goldberg (2002), if the information cost regarding the value of the property is high, the potential buyer becomes reluctant to bear the cost, considering the various possibilities. Such possibilities include: 1) if the seller refuses to sell after the inspection, related expenses will be forfeited; 2) if the result of the inspection is undesirable and the transaction fails, related expenses will be forfeited, as well.

The above mentality can also explain the factors impeding the resale market in the United Kingdom from functioning efficiently. Fear of forfeiting the expense of housing condition surveys reinforces the tendency of prospective purchasers to rely on the cheapest survey available, which results in a significant percentage of purchasers facing unexpected repairs after purchase. When a survey is conducted after reaching sales agreement, in order to avoid the risk of being refused by the seller, it could result in a significant failed transaction cost if condition-related problems identified in the survey cause agreement to fail.

These factors impeding purchasers from obtaining detailed information about the condition of the housing they intend to purchase, are due to the fact that sales of residential property in these countries are carried out on the basis of the principle of "caveat emptor" – literally, "let the buyer beware". In order to promote vitalisation and improve the efficiency of the resale market, it is necessary to introduce systems based on "caveat vendor", and promote disclosure of information on housing conditions by the seller. The following part shows several cases promoting schemes that require sellers of dwellings to disclose housing condition information (Denmark, France and the United Kingdom).

1.2.1.2. Towards disclosure schemes based on "caveat vendor". In Denmark, sellers have historically been liable for 20 years for any defects not disclosed to the buyer in the contract of sale. The Danish act relating to consumer protection in connection with the acquisition of real property, etc., which entered into force on 1 January 1996, exempted sellers from this liability provided they commissioned a survey report by a state-approved and qualified surveyor and provided an insurance quotation covering any hidden defects not detected by the surveyor. The survey report costs a seller from GBP 300-500 depending on the age and size of the property (Nordic Council of Ministers, 1998; ODPM, 1999). If the physical condition is found defective, the purchaser may be subrogated to the position of the seller in terms of claims which the seller could have made against previous sellers and constructors (Nordic Council of Ministers, 1998). Since the system in Denmark has historically been based on "caveat vendor", conducting a survey and presenting the results actually lead to a reduction of the responsibility as well as the risk undertaken by sellers. Therefore, the above-mentioned information package scheme was introduced in 1996 without strong opposition from stakeholders claiming that it would make the seller incur increased transaction costs (which is usually the case in countries based on "caveat emptor").

As the EU directive (2002/91/EC) on "The Energy Performance of Buildings" requires member states to introduce legislation making owners of buildings provide an energy efficiency certificate at the time of (re)sale from 2006, France intends to expand its information package scheme and include an energy efficiency certificate in the information required by the scheme to be provided at the time of sales agreement (see Box 3.3).

> Box 3.3. **Outline of the housing information package in France**
>
> In order to protect consumers from hidden defects and vitalize the resale market, the French government obliges the seller of housing to provide the purchaser with certain information related to specific concerns. The outline of this information package is as follows.
>
> - The seller must provide diagnostics related to the presence of asbestos, lead (in paint) and termites, as well as information regarding natural and technological risks (as for such natural and technological risks, the effective implementation will begin within a year) at the time of agreement of sale (which precedes the contract of sale).
> - The current diagnostics cost (related to presence of asbestos, lead and termites) amounts to EUR 430-750 in case of a five-room house (100m^2) and EUR 420 in case of a three-room apartment. The obligatory diagnostics are usually carried out by a single expert.
> - Diagnostics of installed gas equipment have been added to the package by the law of 3 January 2003 (relevant technical documents are currently under development).
> - Diagnostics of energy efficiency of buildings, following the EU directive, will be added to the package from 2006.
> - As for rental housing, the owner is required to provide potential tenants with information regarding natural and technological risks (the effective implementation will begin within a year). It will also become obligatory to provide diagnostics of energy efficiency from 2007 and of the presence of lead in paint from 2008.
>
> Source: Based on interview by the OECD Secretariat.

In order to protect consumers from hidden defects and improve the efficiency of the resale market, the UK government introduced the Housing Bill to the House of Commons on 8 December 2003, including a new requirement to produce a Home Information Pack before putting a property on the market. After successfully completing its passage through Parliament, the Bill received Royal Assent on 19 November 2004. The introduction of the Home Information Pack means a shift of the UK housing resale market from "caveat emptor" to "caveat vendor". As in the case of the information package in France, the Home Information Pack will incorporate the energy certificate required by the EU directive (2002/91/EC) on "The Energy Performance of Buildings" (see Box 3.4).

> **Box 3.4. Outline of the Home Information Pack,
> United Kingdom**
>
> The Home Information Pack (HIP), which is a key component of housing policy reforms based on the new Housing Bill, is expected to make home buying and selling more efficient, more certain and consumer-friendly. The outline of the HIP is as follows:
>
> - The Secretary of State will prescribe the form and content of the documents to be included in the Home Information Pack in regulations. The prescribed documents and information must relate to matters connected with the property, or its sale, which would be of interest to potential buyers. Clauses 144(5) and (6) of the bill provide an indicative list of contents of a Home Information Pack.
>
> - HIP will include a home condition report, which describes the physical condition of the property including energy efficiency. The cost of preparing a home condition report for a typical 1930s three-bedroom semi-detached house located in a provincial town is estimated to be around GBP 280.
>
> - Other listed contents in clause 144 include: the title to the property, a register required to be kept by or under any enactment, warranties or guarantees, taxes and service charges related to the property.
>
> Before introducing HIP throughout England and Wales on a mandatory basis from the beginning of 2007, the UK government plans to institute a national voluntary six-month "dry-run" of the HIP beginning in summer 2006, which will give an opportunity for the industry to test its new systems and processes. From 2007, a vendor of any residential property or an estate agent acting on behalf of the vendor will be required to provide the potential buyer a copy of the HIP when they put a property on the market (i.e., make it known that the property is for sale).
>
> Source: Based on interview by the OECD Secretariat and UK ODPM (2003a, 2003b, 2004b).

1.2.1.3. Measures securing credibility and reliability of the information package. To make information tools more effective, it is also essential to improve their reliability and credibility. For instance, in the United Kingdom those who provide the home condition report of the HIP are required to be members of an approved certification scheme. Clause 145(5) of the Housing Bill requires the certification scheme to contain appropriate provision for: 1) ensuring that members of the scheme are qualified by their education, training and experience; 2) ensuring that members of the scheme have in force suitable indemnity insurance; and 3) facilitating the resolution of complaints against members of the scheme. If there is any mistake in collecting the Home Information Pack, either the estate agency or the inspector will be held responsible. Therefore, agencies and inspectors should make use of Professional Indemnity Insurance to cover the professional risks of incurring penalties as a result of such mistakes.

In the case of the French system, the purchaser can claim compensation from those who conduct diagnostics for the consequences of liability in respect to the information they provide. According to the French government, since some problems related to surveyors (*e.g.*, some surveyors having insufficient skills, not having insurance coverage corresponding to their responsibilities, and not being independent from sellers, constructors and agencies) have been revealed, the government is now proposing legislative reform to require surveyors who conduct diagnostics to: 1) meet competence criteria validated by a third party; 2) be independent from sellers, constructors, and agencies for sale and rental; and 3) be insured against liability in respect to the information they provide.

In the case of the Danish scheme, the survey report is prepared by a state-approved and qualified surveyor who carries out the inspection of a property (UK ODPM, 1999). The purchaser can make a claim for compensation against the surveyor for defects which should have been mentioned in the report (Nordic Council of Ministers, 1998).

Thus, all three countries require the surveyor who prepares the information package on housing condition to obtain a certain official qualification (often associated with an indemnity insurance scheme), and have clarified that if there is any mistake in the information package, the surveyor will be held responsible for the related damages, etc. In order for information instruments to work effectively, securing such credibility and reliability of the scheme by government intervention in the market is essential.

1.2.2. Information system to address discrimination in the rental housing market

1.2.2.1. Discrimination in the rental housing market. In many studies the special nature of housing has been pointed out. For instance, from consumers' point of view, it is reported that housing has unique characteristics as a necessary good, as follows:

- It takes a significant proportion of income.
- Relevant decisions occur at irregular intervals and therefore information is poor.
- Costs of poor decisions or changes in the environment impose a significant burden on individuals, especially those at the lower end of income distribution (Whitehead, 1991).

As for information failure in the rental housing market, in addition to the lack of information on the renter's side, there is also the issue of imperfect monitoring by the landlord. Landlords are incapable of properly monitoring the actions, etc., of the renter that affect the probability of default (rent arrears) (Arnott, 1987). All these characteristics linked with lack of financing, information failure and discriminatory lending practices (often due to imperfection of monitoring) make it difficult for the consumer, especially disadvantaged households, to find reasonable rental housing in the market.

For instance, in Japan, empirical data shows the presence of discrimination towards elderly households in the private rental housing market. Using paired testers to measure differences in treatment, it was reported that the amount of property information provided to a person in his 60s was about 30% less than the amount provided to a person in his 30s with the same attributes (single, five times the advertised rent in monthly income, etc.) other than age (Nakagawa, 2003). Behind such discrimination is the fact that many landlords hesitate to let their properties to the elderly for fear that they could soon become ill and unable to pay the rent.

In multi-ethnic countries such as the United States, ethnic minorities often face similar discrimination. Using paired testers to measure differences in treatment, the overall incidence of discrimination at some point in the process of buying or renting a housing unit was 50% or more for black or Hispanic renters or home seekers in the United States (Bogdon, et al., 1997).

Such discrimination and lack of information in the rental housing market make it difficult for households with distinctive needs, such as elderly households, to find appropriate rental housing in the market.

1.2.2.2. Measures addressing discrimination in the rental housing market. To reduce such discrimination mainly due to information failure in the rental housing market, it is essential to provide sufficient information to both renter and landlord sides. For instance, to assist the elderly searching for available rental dwellings, the Japanese government introduced a registration system of Rental Housing Available for the Elderly (RHAE) in 2001 and that of Rental Housing Exclusively for the Elderly (RHEE) in 2005. These measures are expected to encourage landlords to let out dwellings to the elderly, and not only to improve access of the elderly to information related to such dwellings. Such measures are supposed to facilitate the elderly with special needs finding appropriate rental housing, as well as to create a new housing market for the elderly (see Box 3.5).

> **Box 3.5. Registration system of Rental Housing Available for the Elderly (RHAE) and Rental Housing Exclusively for the Elderly (RHEE), Japan**
>
> In order to assist the elderly searching for available rental dwellings, the Japanese government introduced a registration system of Rental Housing Available for the Elderly (RHAE) in 2001, which can be accessed on the web or by asking designated organisations. To reduce the fear of rent arrears and increase the amount of rental housing registered in this database, the Japanese government also introduced a rent debt assurance scheme in 2001, which provides assurance for the landlord on condition that the renter pays the assurance fee. By the end of 2004, basic contracts (which are necessary for rent debt assurance) amounted to 14 783 cases. As a result of such efforts by the government, 68 395 dwellings were registered as RHAE in the database by the end of 2004, which increased to around 80 000 by the end of 2005.
>
> Moreover, at the end of 2005, the government introduced a new registration system of Rental Housing Exclusively for the Elderly (RHEE). Based on the Law Improving Residential Stability for the Elderly, landlords of the RHEE are required to register certain related information. As for the RHEE, besides the information necessary to be registered for the RHAE (*e.g.*, name and address of landlord, location, size, structure and facilities of dwellings, rent, etc.), additional information should be registered, such as clarification of being a RHEE, number of units of RHEE, amount of deposit required when the elderly settle in, outline of common facilities and available daily services (*e.g.*, bathing, dining, toilet assistance) and amount of pre-paid rents. By 14 February 2006, 1 266 dwellings have been registered as RHEE.
>
> Source: Based on interview by the OECD Secretariat.

1.2.3. Toward effective information instruments to vitalise the housing market

As seen above, information instruments play a key role in enhancing the efficiency of the housing market and thereby vitalising market activities. Experience in some countries shows that in order for those instruments to work effectively, it is imperative to design and implement the system carefully by, for instance, transforming schemes based on "caveat emptor" to schemes based on "caveat vendor". In addition, securing credibility and reliability of the scheme is essential for it to work effectively.

Moreover, information instruments have the potential not only to improve housing affordability of disadvantaged households but also to contribute to creating a new market which has not been recognised by market players. Therefore, promotion of these measures in the housing market should be one of the key concerns in future housing policies. Governments should play an important role in establishing the foundation on which these information instruments could work effectively towards more efficient functioning of the market.

1.3. Privatisation and decentralisation in social housing policy

1.3.1. Policy shift in social rented housing sector towards market-oriented approach

After the Second World War, during which millions of dwellings were destroyed and damaged, governments in many OECD countries intervened in their housing markets to compensate for the huge shortage of housing. The social rented housing sector was assigned a prominent role in the efforts to accelerate new housing construction, and the 1950s and 1960s formed the heyday of social housing in many countries, with heavy subsidies and rent controls.

In some countries, this sector continued to thrive throughout the 1970s (Great Britain) and on into the 1980s (Sweden and the Netherlands). But at some point after the peak, many governments began to reconsider the position of the social rented housing sector (Priemus, et al., 1997). As soon as housing markets returned to normal and the home-owner sector picked up, it seemed that the share of social housing could be much smaller, with reduction of the heavy burden of public expenditure. During the 1980s and 1990s, many countries observed a housing policy shift away from government control and towards market forces, coupled with reduced levels of government support and greater independence of the private housing sector, which was part of a more general trend towards privatisation and decentralisation of public services.

In the United Kingdom, public housing policy was drastically changed through the introduction of "right to buy (RTB)" schemes which promoted privatisation of public housing. Since the mid-1970s British housing policy has been dominated by two factors: the need to reduce public expenditure and the ideological desire to expand home ownership (Brown, et al., 1997). The Housing Act (1980), which introduced a statutory obligation on local authorities to administer a right to buy for sitting tenants, was envisaged as an efficient means of achieving these objectives. Under the terms of the Act, public sector tenants were given the right to purchase their rented dwellings at a discount relating to the total length of time they had been tenants. The RTB helped to open up homeownership to some 1.5 million households in England (Figure 3.2). Since homeownership is generally regarded as contributing to enhancing stability, social responsibility and civic involvement, the RTB has been considered as one of the most successful housing policies during the period of 1975-2000 (UK ODPM, 2005).

Figure 3.2. **Number of right to buy sales, England, 1980-2001**

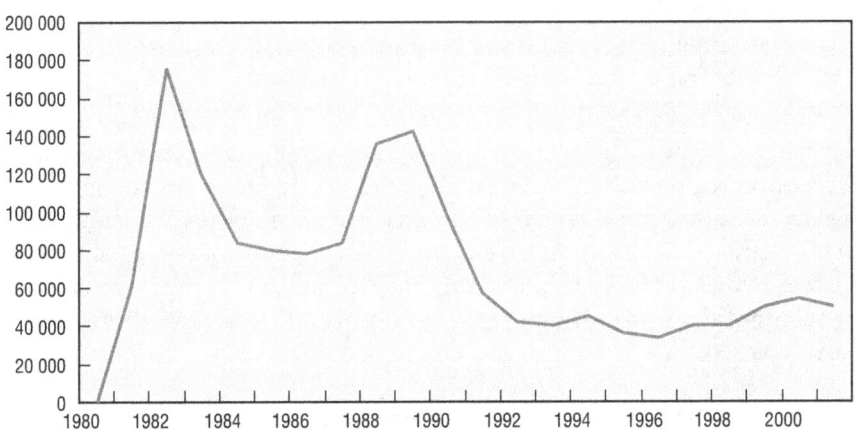

Source: UK ODPM (2005), Lessons from the Past, Challenges for Future for Housing Policy, UK Office of the Deputy Prime Minister, London.

In the Netherlands, the social rented sector had been expanded by various measures such as subsidies and rent control since the Second World War; and at the end of the 1980s, public housing expenses were very high and the social rented housing stock represented 40% of the market, a larger share that in any other OECD countries (Priemus, 1998). However, the perception of how the social rented sector should function changed drastically in the 1980s. This change occurred in response to the need to cut back on government expenditure, which put pressure on the field of housing (Van Kempen, et al., 1999). In 1989, the government announced fundamental changes in housing policy in the government's White Paper "Housing in the 1990s", which paved the way for market-oriented housing policy. Broadly, the changes can be described as four directions: 1) decentralisation of housing policy by giving responsibility to housing associations and municipal governments; 2) abolition of construction and operating subsidies for social-rented dwellings; 3) stricter targeting of housing allowances towards lower-income households; and 4) promotion of home ownership by keeping mortgage payments fully-deductible (Dieleman, 1999).

One of the important results from this policy-shift was that the independence of housing associations was strengthened. It gave the housing associations, which own over 99% of the social housing stock, more freedom in housing production and selling properties, as well as in the field of rent-setting in the existing stock. Moreover, in 1995, the "grossing and balancing" agreement largely dissolved the financial ties binding the social rented sector and the central government. Under this agreement, housing associations repaid all their outstanding government loans. At the same time, the associations received a lump sum amounting to the estimated value of all government subsidy obligations (Dieleman, 1999). Housing associations are required to finance maintenance from their operating budgets and reserves, and to borrow on the capital market for new construction.

On the other hand, home ownership was promoted by keeping mortgage payments fully deductible. The reasons for supporting home ownership range form encouraging citizen responsibility and family life to encouraging self-realisation, privacy and capital formation (Social and Cultural Planning Office of the Netherlands, 2000). As a result of the restructuring of the social housing system as well as measures promoting home ownership, home ownership has been increasing rapidly, especially among high-income households (see Table 3.3).

Table 3.3. **Proportion of owner-occupied housing, per income distribution quartile and household type, 1982-1998 (in %)**

Household type	Income distribution	1982	1986	1990	1994	1998
Head (with children)	1st quartile (low income)	20	17	17	18	17
	2nd quartile	20	19	16	26	28
	3rd quartile	35	34	33	47	47
	4th quartile (high income)	45	57	55	61	59
	Total	24	22	23	27	26
Head + partner (with children)	1st quartile (low income)	39	39	40	48	49
	2nd quartile	30	28	30	36	44
	3rd quartile	39	42	42	57	64
	4th quartile (high income)	58	60	66	75	80
	Total	44	46	51	58	65
total		42	43	45	48	50

Note: Distinction is made between households with one head (single-person households and single-parent families) and households with two heads (couples and families with children).
Source: Social and Cultural Planning Office of the Netherlands (2000), *Social and Cultural Report 2000: The Netherlands in a European Perspective,* Social and Cultural Planning Office of the Netherlands.

1.3.2. Unintended consequences from the market-oriented approach

As seen above, although policy reform of social housing systems towards market orientation has achieved initial goals, such as raising the level of home ownership, it also caused other consequences which were not initially intended. One of these consequences was concentration of disadvantaged households in the social housing sector, or spatial concentration of those households in certain areas (i.e., residential segregation).

In the United Kingdom, the RTB scheme led to the decline of public housing. Figure 3.3 shows the trend of housing tenure in England. While home ownership has been increasing in England throughout the 20th century, the decrease in social renters in the 1980s is attributed to the RTB scheme.

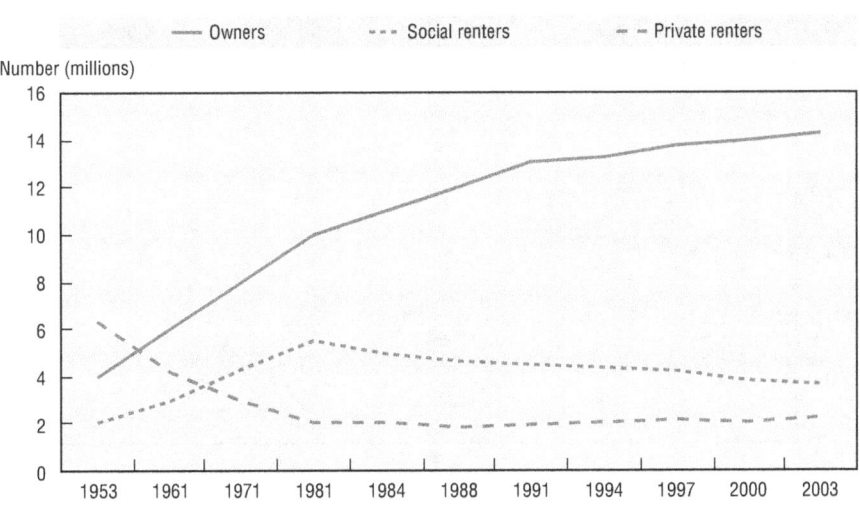

Figure 3.3. **Trends of tenure in England**

Source: UK ODPM (2004a), *Housing in England 2002/3: A Report Principally from the 2002/2003 Survey of English Housing*, UK Office of the Deputy Prime Minister, London.

Meusen, et al., (1995) point out that the combination of measures taken to increase owner-occupancy, such as the cut-back on subsidies for supply of social housing, increasing the rents of existing social housing stock, and the introduction of Right to Buy legislation, led to a dramatic change in the socio-economic nature of social rental tenants. As a result of these measures, the increase of low-income and the decrease of high-income groups in the social rented sector has become much more prominent in Britain. Adjusted for size, the British social rented sector now houses a much greater concentration of households from the lowest income deciles compared to other European countries (Figure 3.4). While the RTB was successful in raising the level of home-ownership, it has been criticised for contributing to this phenomenon of so-called "residualisation" of the social rented sector. "Residualisation" describes the tendency for the sector to house a greater concentration of the poorest and most disadvantaged households.

Moreover, the level of sales of the RTB scheme has been much higher on popular estates where housing demand is strong. Few sales have taken place in the least desirable estates, particularly those that comprise only apartments, not houses (Best, 1996). This phenomenon has been observed since the early stage of implementation of the scheme. Sewel, et al. (1984) monitored the pattern of council house sales and pointed out that semi-detached and terraced properties sold at a greater rate than flatted properties, and estates with higher socio-economic status and a higher popularity rating experienced a greater level of sales, concluding that a continued policy of

Figure 3.4. **Representation of income groups in social rented housing**

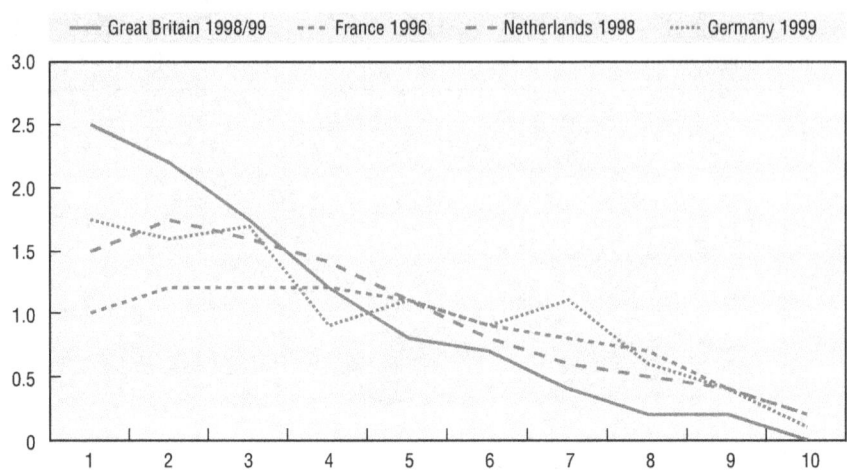

Note: The percentage of households in each income decile is divided by the size of the social rented sector. If 10% of people in the lowest income decile, and 10% of the housing stock is socially rented, the figure is one. Figures above one represent over-representation and those below one under-representation.

Source: UK ODPM (2005), *Lessons from the Past, Challenges for Future for Housing Policy*, UK Office of the Deputy Prime Minister, London.

unrestricted sales would have a deleterious effect on the quality of the stock available to rent and would increase the pressure towards a residualisation of public sector housing. This tendency has facilitated the spatial concentration of disadvantaged households, namely, residential segregation. Various studies suggest that residential segregation aggravates the social exclusion of residents in these areas from mainstream economic activities by creating barriers to jobs, education and other services, and undermines social stability as well as sustainable urban economic development.

In the Netherlands, since the promotion of home ownership pushed better-off households into home-ownership, the proportion of households with high incomes served by the social rented sector decreased dramatically during the 1990s (see Figure 3.5), which led to the residualisation of the social rented sector. Moreover, in the construction of new housing, the stress shifted from the social rented sector to the private market sector, where the owner-occupied sector flourished. New construction was promoted in the more expensive parts of the housing market, while the supply of inexpensive dwellings was expected to be made available by a filtering process, resulting from moves of higher income households from inexpensive to more expensive dwellings. Moreover, housing associations, which have major social housing tasks, but at the same time have to safeguard their financial continuity and have to bear numerous financial risks themselves, are giving thought to

Figure 3.5. **Form of housing tenure in the Netherlands by income decile, 1981-2002**

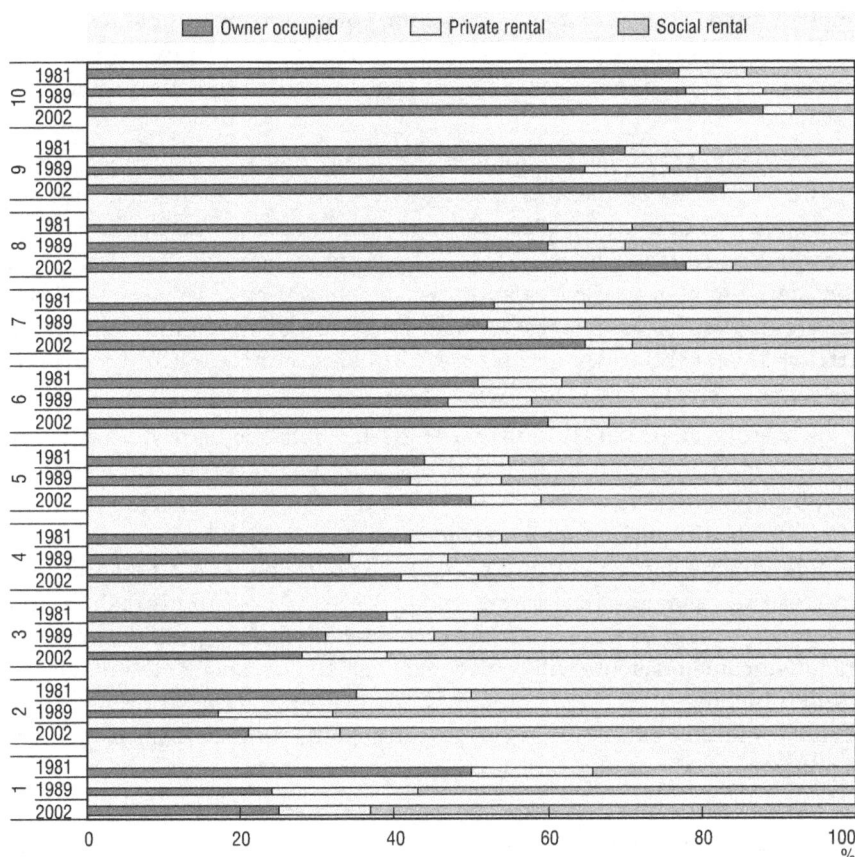

Source: Elsinga, Marja, Marietta Haffner, and Harry van der Heijden (2005), "A Unitary Rental Market in Netherlands?: Theoretical Exploration and Empirical Evidence", paper presented at the ENHR conference "Housing in Europe – New Challenges and Innovations in Tomorrow's Cities", 29 June-3 July 2005, Reykjavik.

selectively selling off dwellings and to strengthening their financial positions. These trends are facilitating the spatial concentration of disadvantaged households in social rented housing estates.

1.3.3. *New policy directions to address emerging issues*

To address these unintended consequences, such as residential segregation, various measures have been implemented in each country. The main concern in tackling residential segregation is how to promote social mix by attracting or retaining populations that would contribute to consolidation of the social and economic profile of distressed areas with a high percentage of social rental housing. While traditional measures promoting social mix such as area redevelopment and upgrades of existing housing stock have been implemented, an emerging challenge for policy makers is how to achieve social values such as promotion of social mix in the context of pursuing market orientation, which was already set as a main direction of housing policy.

In the United Kingdom, although the idea of area redevelopment itself is not new and in earlier periods housing redevelopment meant public housing construction, in recent decades, the importance of the private sector's role in contributing to redevelopment has been more recognised. This attitude is considered to be a new policy approach to achieve social values by utilising private market forces. Moreover, it has also been identified that, in order to attract investors and promote new housing construction by private developers, "critical mass" is a key concern.

Quercia, et al. (1997) contend that the number of middle-income households residing in a given area must exceed a certain threshold for significant benefits to accrue. In this case, threshold is defined as the point after which a change in an expected benefit, associated with a change in middle-income settlement in a particular geographic area, is significantly greater than that predicted by a linear projection. At the threshold, the marginal increase in an expected benefit resulting from a given increment in middle-income residents will be noticeably greater because of the number of middle income households already present in the area. In other words, "critical mass" – exceeding a certain threshold – is necessary to achieve significant social benefits.

In Newcastle, the concept of "critical mass" is considered a key concern in area redevelopment. A new city-wide regeneration strategy to the year 2020, "Going for Growth: A Green Paper", was adopted by Newcastle City Council in July 1999, the core of which was large-scale housing redevelopment primarily concerned with introducing a new, more middle-class population into these areas, by building new houses and demolishing existing dwellings. Mostly, these were in areas of council housing, and in their place, new housing would be constructed by private developers and registered social landlords (Byrne, 2000). In the presentation of Going for Growth, it was constantly reiterated that, in order to succeed, the redevelopment and new building would have to be on a sufficient scale. The scale of new development was seen as critical to give investors confidence and attract both their investments and developers (Cameron, 2003). This is because the scale of new development was seen as critical to making the new neighbourhoods attractive to more middle-class newcomers. It was necessary to bring in a new population on a sufficient scale to change substantially the social mix of school catchments, so that middle-class families would be willing to send their children to local schools. While low-rent neighbourhoods of German, Dutch and French cities still have a certain number of middle- and even higher-income households which provide a source of demand for new, higher-cost housing within the neighbourhoods, low-income households are more concentrated in low-rent neighbourhoods in the United Kingdom (see Table 3.4). As a result, the success of the housing redevelopment policy largely depends on the possibility of attracting a new population from outside the area. In order to revitalise the deeply stigmatised areas, Going for Growth relies on critical mass, i.e., the creation of new neighbourhoods and populations large enough to challenge the stigmatised image, to create a sense of security and to transform both the demand for services and the catchment populations of neighbourhood schools. To achieve critical mass, the private sector is expected to play a key role, with its innovative thinking, in attracting new middle-income populations.

Table 3.4. **Development of distribution of households in social housing, 1980s-1990s**

	Income deciles 1-3		Income deciles 4-7		Income deciles 8-10	
	1980s	1990s	1980s	1990s	1980s	1990s
The Netherlands (1989-93)	42.9	44.3	42.8	42.4	14.3	13.3
Germany (1982-93)	33.2	44.0	44.7	42.5	22.1	13.5
UK (1988-96)	59.1	61.8	31.9	33.5	9.0	4.7
France (1988-92)	37.3	38.2	46.6	45.5	16.1	15.9
Belgium (1988-92)	55.6	52.4	31.2	34.6	13.2	13.0
Sweden (1990-95)	39.7	49.0	45.0	45.0	15.3	10.5

Source: Van der Heijden, Harry (2002), "Social Rented Housing in Western Europe: Developments and Expectations", *Urban Studies*, Vol. 39, No. 2, pp. 327-340.

In the Netherlands, to make meeting the housing needs of the neediest and maintaining appropriate social balance within social housing estates compatible under increased administrative and financial independence, housing associations are paying much more attention to the development of "strategic asset management". Asset management is concerned with an analysis of the performance of an organisation's assets in support of decisions about holding, selling and repositioning. While the emphasis in private-sector asset management is on optimising financial performance, in the social rented sector, financial performance is not the primary criterion for management decisions. The key question for social landlords is how to reach their social housing objectives efficiently (Gruis, et al., 2004). For instance, front-runners such as Delftwonen have formulated quantitative goals for the development and performance of their housing stock (see Table 3.5).

Table 3.5. **Housing stock development goals (Delftwonen, the Netherlands)**

Aspect	Goal
Investments	Replacement of 330 cheap flats with lift
	Replacement of 670 cheap flats without lift
	Upgrading of 660 flats
	Adjustment of 660 homes for the elderly
	Adjustment of 250 single-family dwellings
	Upgrading of 250 single-family dwellings for families
Affordability	All dwellings for younger households
(Minimum percentage of dwellings affordable with housing allowance)	80% of the dwellings for the elderly
	50% of other dwellings
Special target groups	Provide 50% of the local housing need of special groups (such as handicapped people)
Desired differentiation of quality	Basic: 30%
	Standard: 60%
	Luxurious: 10%
Maximum number of sales	3 000 homes

Source: Gruis, Vincent, Nico Nieboer and Andrew Thomas (2004), "Strategic Asset Management in the Social Rented Sector: Approaches of Dutch and English Housing Associations", Urban Studies, Vol. 41, No. 7, pp. 1229-1248.

While a wide range of strategies is considered and applied, diversification of the price and quality of dwellings within the portfolio according to housing demand is considered a central theme in strategic asset management. To attract or retain populations that would contribute to consolidation of the social and economic profile of distressed areas, providing diverse options for demand in the housing market is considered to be essential (see Box 3.6).

Thus, many associations are trying to promote tenure diversification by presenting various tenure options so that existing tenants could choose the most appropriate option meeting their housing needs, which is expected to contribute to maintaining a diverse population profile by retaining better-off households. One of the key challenges for housing associations is now becoming how to achieve social goals with full consideration of the choice of consumers in the housing market.

1.3.4. Towards social values achievement through market mechanisms

Experience in some countries shows that new policy approaches are emerging in new circumstances where it is becoming a challenge for policy makers to address social issues such as residential segregation in the context of market orientation, such as privatisation and decentralisation. The way government interacts with the market is now becoming substantially important.

> **Box 3.6. "Client's choice" programme, Woonbron-Maasoevers, the Netherlands**
>
> The housing association, Woonbron-Maasœvers, in Rotterdam, is experimenting with a programme in which, for a part of the housing stock, tenants are given the choice of five tenure options.
>
> - Normal rent contract;
> - Fixed rent contract for five or ten years;
> - Fixed rent-increase contract for five or ten years;
> - Purchase, with a discount on the market value and a sale-back guarantee with a 50:50 division of increase or decrease in value between the association and the tenant;
> - Outright purchase, under the condition that the association has the right to buy at market value when the tenant sells the dwelling.
>
> Several associations have followed this experiment and many other associations have adopted parts of this approach.
>
> Source: Gruis, Vincent, Nico Nieboer and Andrew Thomas (2004), "Strategic Asset Management in the Social Rented Sector: Approaches of Dutch and English Housing Associations", *Urban Studies*, Vol. 41, No. 7, pp. 1229-1248.

For instance, in order to address residential segregation in stigmatised areas by area redevelopment, "critical mass", *i.e.*, the creation of new neighbourhoods and populations large enough to challenge the stigmatised image, is considered to be essential, but which cannot easily be achieved only by market forces. While critical mass is imperative to give private investors confidence and attract both their investments and developers, the private sector's innovative way of appealing to the choice of better-off households is important to attract them into redevelopment areas and achieve critical mass. Governments should demonstrate strong leadership and play a key role in organising private activities to achieve such critical mass.

From the social housing sector's view point, it is also becoming a key challenge to achieve social goals by appealing to the choice of market players. For instance, in order to attract or retain populations that would contribute to improving the social and economic profile of distressed areas, offering diverse options according to various preferences in the housing market is becoming one of the strategies in social housing asset management.

Privatisation and decentralisation are important market-oriented directions for utilising market forces and its efficiency to achieve certain policy objectives. However, there are issues which cannot be addressed simply by the withdrawal of the public sector from the market. Since it is obvious that going back to the old role of governments as direct providers or regulators is not a desirable future direction, the new role the public sector plays in interacting with the market to achieve social values is crucial for the future market-oriented approach.

Conclusion

A market-oriented approach has been one of the prominent trends in building and housing policy in recent decades, which can be described as a move away from the role of government as direct producer, to a new role as enabler, facilitating and encouraging private building and housing activities through market mechanisms, coupled with reduced levels of government support and greater independence of the building and housing sector. Mainly against the background of the pressure to reduce public expenditure, many governments have pursued this approach through various measures to achieve their policy objectives.

In pursuing the market-oriented approach, one of the key concerns is how to enhance the efficiency of the market, and, in many countries, governments have intervened in the market for this purpose through various measures, such as regulatory reform and promotion of information instruments. Improving the flexibility of the regulatory systems is essential to promote private sector innovation and creativity while attempting to achieve initial objectives, such as addressing obstacles hindering efficient functioning of the market. In addition, information instruments play a key role in vitalising market activities and improving the efficiency of the market. However, experience in some countries suggests that careful implementation is required to enable these measures to work effectively in the market. For instance, innovative regulatory reforms cannot be accomplished simply by imposing them on the market. To make regulatory reforms work effectively in the market, the role governments play in enhancing their adaptability to the market is imperative. In addition, governments play an important role in establishing the foundation on which various instruments, such as information tools, could work effectively by, for instance, enhancing the reliability of these instruments.

Furthermore, it is now becoming evident that there are issues that cannot be addressed only by efficient market functionality, or, in some cases, are aggravated by certain types of market-oriented approach. For instance, some countries have pursued privatisation or decentralisation of the social rented housing sector and promoted market-oriented housing policy to utilise market forces and their efficiency for housing provision. This shift in housing policy has attained its initial goals such as raising the level of home ownership and could be evaluated as successful in its own terms. However, this shift has also caused or accelerated unintended outcomes such as residential segregation which would aggravate the social exclusion of residents in certain areas. While these social issues cannot be addressed simply by the withdrawal of the public sector from the market, it is obvious that going back to the old role of governments as direct providers or regulators is not a desirable future direction. In these new circumstances, how to re-orient the market-oriented approach is becoming a challenge for policy makers. Experience in some countries shows that new policy approaches are emerging in this situation, such as achieving "critical mass" in area redevelopment by utilising the private sector's innovative ways to appeal to the choice of market players, and strategic asset management with full consideration of market preferences. The key question in the new approach is how to achieve social goals through well-designed interaction with market choices or preferences. The new role the public sector plays in interacting with the market is crucial for the future market-oriented approach.

To help regions realise their full potential and achieve sustainable development, market forces play a key role, and the market-oriented approach is essential in future policy direction. In pursuing this approach, it is becoming a great challenge for policy makers not only to enable the market to function more efficiently but also to achieve social goals through market mechanisms as much as possible. Lessons from some countries show that key questions are how to internalise market players' behaviour in designing and implementing policy measures, and how to enhance the adaptability of these measures to the market, as well as how to establish the foundation on which these measures can work effectively. The way governments interact with the market is now becoming significantly important for re-orienting the market-oriented approach.

Notes

1. Akerlof (1970) provides the classic example in his analysis of the used car market, describing the interplay between uncertainty and differentiated quality in the presence of asymmetric information. Assuming that suppliers are divided between those who offer low quality ("lemons") and high-quality used cars, adverse selection favours the sellers of "lemons", who will exploit their information advantage over the buyers. If buyers are incapable of telling the difference between a good and a bad car, bad cars drive out the good cars by selling at the same price. Therefore, if the buyer does not have access to the information necessary to evaluate the quality of the commodity, the seller has incentives to put low-quality commodities on the market. The bias towards the sale of commodities with defects would ultimately undermine the market for that commodity altogether.

2. When HPIS first started in 2000, it was only applied to newly constructed housing.

ISBN 978-92-64-02240-9
OECD Territorial Review
Competitive Cities
A New Entrepreneurial Paradigm in Spatial Develompent
© OECD 2007

Chapter 4

Spatial Planning for Competitiveness

> *Urban spatial planning in OECD countries has recently undergone major rethinking, characterised by a resurgence of strategic planning and the broadening of goals. It has also evolved into a more network-based and collaborative mode of planning with the participation of new partners, especially the private sector. This chapter illustrates these trends, based on a number of examples, and casts light on the challenges in tackling fragmentation by upgrading local planners' expertise.*

Introduction

While spatial planning systems in all countries continue to pursue the same objectives: promoting long-term territorial development, co-ordinating government functions through land use and physical investment and ensuring the planning of sectoral activities, they are nevertheless undergoing major transformations.

Traditionally, spatial development policies were articulated in master or development plans. The emphasis in such plans often turned to the promotion of various projects and to a focus on land use, but in a situation where spatial dynamics were not adequately taken into account. Spatial planning often ended up being strategy-less, imposing a rigid pattern of zoned land uses. This experience is increasingly seen as being counterproductive in a context of globalisation of production and trade and correlative increased competition between regions and cities.

A new competitiveness agenda is now driving, to a large extent, member countries' policies for planning. Metropolitan and regional economies are more dependent on their position in global networks than on the traditional powers and investments. The ability to develop and to stimulate competitiveness is becoming a central consideration in a number of countries. In that context, a new role is devolved to spatial planning, which is becoming more strategic, notably with regard to infrastructure investment and location of business activities. New strategic planning also highlights other goals: 1) the importance of cultural assets in attracting skilled workers in the new knowledge industries, as well as tourists; 2) environmental sustainability, reflecting new conservation priorities and new ways of thinking about the flow of people, goods and waste products; and 3) social cohesion, thus leading to concern for the quality and accessibility of particular resources, amenities and opportunities in the city and region.

These changes have been accompanied by a growing integration of areas and localities in the same functional regions, thus leading to a greater involvement of sub-national levels in territorial planning. Spatial planning systems have also evolved into a more network-based and flexible structure with closer collaboration between levels of government. Since the 1980s, the main public and private stakeholders of most metropolitan regions have attempted to improve their co-operation and collaboration within their regions in order to strengthen the conditions for competitiveness.

On the practical level, spatial strategies are shifting emphasis from imposing restrictions to promoting development. This often translates into less-detailed regulation by central government, increasing the indicative (non-binding) aspect of planning and providing greater latitude for other levels of government, public citizens and market stakeholders, in an effort to stimulate growth.

These new trends towards entrepreneurialism and economic growth are highlighted in Section 1, using the examples of several major cities. To respond to the new competitiveness challenges, many governments have changed their approach, increasing the focus on development and deregulation. Planning has become increasingly strategic (Section 2). The involvement of new actors and the often-fragmented nature of metropolitan governance have triggered institutional changes, in particular the development of partnerships, and rendered local planning more complex. This trend has also been strengthened by the growing autonomy granted to lower levels of government to implement urban planning and influence space management. While entrepreneurial planning has had recourse to new instruments, it is nevertheless facing intrinsic problems. One important issue is bridging the gap between citizen and client demand and project supply. Another is linked to the capabilities of local planners to increase their expertise and to upgrade their planning skills (Section 3).

1. The development of urban planning in several major cities: evidence of the changing role of spatial planning

1.1. *The competitiveness agenda*

Globalisation has markedly altered the role of metropolitan regions. Today, large cities act as commercial, industrial, and service hubs. Accordingly, they play a key role in building national competitiveness. Metropolitan regions host the most advanced industries (*e.g.*, biotechnology, ICT, fashion and design); they are thus producing the larger part of the national added-value by concentrating capital investment and skill resources and taking full advantage of industrial diversity and agglomeration effects.

Cities compete to attract and retain mobile factors of production, namely labour and capital. They compete directly with each other, providing the greatest quantity or optimal combination of location factors (such as green spaces, affordable housing, business-support, quality of pre-university education for families, presence of headquarters' functions, etc.) to lure skilled labour and investment. However, some argue that this competition is indirect, as well, deriving from competition among businesses. Whatever one's view on city competition, policies to enhance the capacities of cities to attract businesses and workers have shaped regional and local policy in many OECD countries.

Cities are often ranked according to criteria such as GDP per capita, and urban policies assessed accordingly. Empirical evidence shows that spatial policies have in many cases delivered positive results. In just a few decades, a number of urban regions that were in poor socio-economic condition, because of deindustrialisation and high unemployment rates, have succeeded in restoring their local economy and becoming competitive once again. Such is the case of Barcelona (see below), Dublin or Budapest. Often, a local (spatial) strategy aimed at providing a better organisation to the city, or supporting a local specialisation, is at the origin of the recovery.

1.2. New trends in urban planning: some city examples

This need for a vision and an urban strategy is reflected in the shift of attitude among a majority of city and national planners towards urban entrepreneurialism. The last decades have, in fact, seen considerable transformations in spatial planning in most countries. "From the 1950s to the 1970s, clear goals and models were indispensable elements of local urban development planning. Organisationally, they were embodied in autonomous institutions, new urban development offices or in relevant interfaces." At the national level, planning was conceived as aiming at guiding and regulating the location of investment and at providing a range of city services such as education, housing and public transportation. This system was nevertheless criticised for its lack of flexibility, its rigid control and for its inadequate transparency.

"The late-1970s saw a turnabout. It became necessary to recognise the complexity of cities. Planning was often reinterpreted as a process of continuous learning and of proceeding gradually, to ensure transparent goal-setting." The idea was to avoid adopting goals that would merely project present conditions into the future (Bock, 2006). In some countries, city authorities saw their role as providers of collective services declining, as the result of budget-cuts, privatisation and restructuring.

However, this "project-oriented, incrementalist" style of planning soon ran out of breath. Recent demands for local planning process now favor the resumption of a more strategic orientation. At the national level, planning instruments have regained popularity. The new model is nevertheless different from the one which prevailed in the 1960s and 1970s, providing communication opportunities and evaluation frameworks at the city level. Cities, in turn, started to take a more proactive attitude, in which business expansion and inward investment are directly promoted. In many areas, increasing emphasis on large projects and the development of particular districts have now resulted in a greater involvement of corporate actors. City governments and local businesses are drawn into closer co-operation (through public-private partnerships arising from their mutual self-interest in the promotion of local economic development). The emergence of this entrepreneurial model and its characteristics are further detailed in Table 4.1.

Table 4.1. **Trends in spatial planning**

	Traditional planning approach (managerial)	Transitional approach (incrementalist)	New planning approach (strategic)
Main goals	Allocation of land	Spatial redevelopment and infrastructure growth	Economic development, environmental and social sustainability
Concepts (dynamics)	Implementation and tactics	Opened planning	Strategic vision
Functions	Provision of public services	Focus on project	Promoting innovation, risk-taking and development
Substantive aspects or forms (static)	Center/periphery rationale	Redevelopment of city centres, strengthening rural/urban linkages	Polycentricity, urban corridors
Actors	Public actors	Involvement of the private sector	A broad set of stakeholders, numerous PPP
Regional and local dimensions	Hierarchical relationships between central, regional and local; central control	Emerging role of regions	Strategic aspects increasingly decentralised

This change of paradigm has permeated many cities in the United States. Firstly, it is in the United States that the so-called smart-growth movement has thrived. To a large extent, this movement could be considered a precursor of the entrepreneurial approach in planning. The Portland area was one of the first to establish an elected metropolitan government, Portland Metro. This agency subsequently elaborated a new 2040 metropolitan plan that permitted a forecast increase of 50% in regional population to be accommodated. The term "smart growth" was actually first used in the late-1980s, in recognition of the strategy-making process in Massachussetts. Rather than managing and restricting growth, as earlier growth management systems had done, smart growth was meant to connote a pro-growth orientation. Secondly, it is traditional in the United States to develop urban strategic planning involving a wide variety of local stakeholders, including businesses, banks, universities, and local authorities. In that context, a growing number of metropolitan areas, including New York, San Diego or Boston, have adopted or are preparing new comprehensive regional plans.

While commonplace in the United States, the involvement of the private sector in planning is relatively recent in Europe. For a long time, planning was the responsibility of central government, and if planning was delegated to lower levels, it nevertheless operated in a hierarchical manner. As emphasised above, this is changing, giving way to a new entrepreneurial model, although at different rates according to the city and country. Among the most interesting examples of this new model, one can cite:

- *Barcelona: (private sector-based urban dynamic)*: In this city, during the 1990s, standard spatial planning was mainly based on redevelopment of brownfields (*e.g.*, parks, social facilities) and involved private developers for housing programmes in the same way as was done for the construction of the Olympic village. Planning implementation remained, nevertheless, loosely linked with the General Metropolitan Plans. The rather technical and architectural approach followed was increasingly superseded at the end of the millenium by a more strategic mode of planning. This new model can be equated to a kind of urban corporate planning around a core of economic and competitiveness-development goals, with certain social and environmental objectives attached. This entrepreneurial approach has been further developed through increasing recourse to the private sector and public-private partnerships (PPP), taking advantage of the culture of public-private partnerships already existing at the time of the Olympic Games (1992).

- *London (the emergence of metropolitan planning)*: In the capital, the transformation of the planning system followed a change in governance in the region. After the abolition of the Greater London Council, a special committee was created to prepare strategic planning guidance. However, this exercise was relatively symbolic. These guidance principles were only broad orientations, contained in documents of only a few pages. Strategic planning was in fact revived in 1997 with the change of government. A new mayor was elected and a Greater London Authority (GLA) was created to take over existing "Quangos" with some devolution of power from the central government. The Mayor elaborated a Spatial Development Strategy (SDS) with a wide mandate, including economic development, regeneration, environment, retail waste management, etc. The SDS is underpinned by sub-regional development frameworks established in partnership between the GLA, boroughs and other stakeholders. An important consideration is the attempt to make London more accountable to its citizens, while allowing leadership and vision that fully exploit its comparative advantages. It is believed that appropriate policies can achieve consensus, and even reinforce the entrepreneurial approach. The concept followed is, thus, comprehensive involvement of many stakeholders with a large range of innovative approaches to participation. The business sector is a driving force in these partnerships and through its London Business Board is able to significantly influence the competitiveness agenda.

- *Vienna (soft strategic planning and significant private sector involvement)*: Following the collapse of the Berlin Wall and the changing geopolitical situation, Vienna's urban development experienced a new dynamism. The burst of development was reflected in an increasing demand for both accommodation and workspace, caused by increasing immigration and lack of well-equipped offices. In addition, many international enterprises chose Vienna as their principal headquarters to open up eastern European markets. In 1998, a new strategic plan was outlined, focusing on innovation, knowledge and high quality of life. This plan was not binding, but it inaugurated a more open planning policy, notably with the abolition of the limit on high-rise buildings, which facilitated the financial commitment of individual investors, as well as international investment groups. In the context of a growing demand for offices in the densely-built area, more attention was paid to economic development. Two of the three main poles of urban development, Wienerberg City and Millenium City were inspired and financed by the private sector. Within the public sector, however, cooperation between the city (which is also a province) and the suburbs (belonging to another province) has been limited.[1]

These different examples do not pretend to constitute *per se* an exhaustive sample of large cities, but they pinpoint several important trends:

- They confirm the emergence or resurgence of strategic spatial planning as a driving force to integrate territorial performance and quality goals in spatial policy. It appears that strategic plans can be more or less sophisticated, with data-collection and in-depth analysis of comparative advantages, or characterised by a more general conceptual content.

- Partnering between municipalities has increased to better take advantage of the growing polycentric nature of metropolitan regions. These partnerships have also extended to integrate numerous other actors and institutions: agencies, private sector, and semi-public bodies, in order to augment the number of projects and their innovative potential. Through the mobilisation of a large range of actors it becomes possible to tap knowledge resources from many stakeholders.

- A number of planning problems have also been stressed: the often relatively loose relationship between metropolitan strategies and particular projects (Barcelona, Vienna), the tension between the central government and the metropolitan authorities (London), or the fragmentation of planning resulting from administrative borders (Vienna).

To deepen the analysis and improve understanding of the policy implications of the entrepreneurial model, it is proposed to focus on the three main topics stressed above: the change in spatial policies induced by the spread of strategic planning, the new aspects of policy delivery linked with the new planning governance (i.e., the emergence of collaborative and network-based planning) and future prospects, given the need to face increasing local conflicts and to manage more complex planning.

2. Strategic planning policies and frameworks

Strategic planning, after being eclipsed in most countries during the 1980s, has come back to the fore at the end of the millennium. The competitiveness agenda has been one of the main reasons for this resumption of interest, together with the "search for spatial forms and relationships having the potential to promote new goals such as sustainable development" (Healey, 2004). This has led to a theoretical rethinking of the planning process, emphasising the focus on a limited number of key issues, a more realistic long-term perspective, an effort to generate new ideas and often the incorporation of monitoring, feedback and revision. Planning practices have, nevertheless, not necessarily reached all these goals. In general strategic planning, policies have encountered certain limits. For example, they often failed to significantly reduce sprawl or the proliferation of peripheries (Monclus, 2003).

2.1. Reinventing strategic planning

Strategic planning is not new, but the way it has been done recently differs from the past. First, it has become prevalent at different levels: local, regional, national, trans-national and supra-national. Because of this multiplicity of territorial levels, their nesting at metropolitan and local levels has become less and less straightforward. At the same time, central government strategic frameworks, at least in unitary countries, have become more indicative and conceptual. Second, plans are now broader in scope, combining physical development objectives with less tangible goals. Third, strategic planning needs to take into account functional areas and the moving borders of cities.

2.1.1. Improving forward-looking analysis and frameworks

An important aim of strategic plans and frameworks is to provide city stakeholders, planners and developers with a better understanding of the critical relationships which are likely to shape the future economic, social and environmental characteristics of a place and boost the competitiveness of cities and metropolitan regions. Spatial planning issues need to be examined in a prospective manner (Albrechts, 2001). Such an approach emphasises a number of (mega-) trends and points to their implications for cities.[2]

It also means that a sufficiently long time perspective should be adopted if plans are to be effective in bringing remedies to structural problems and benefiting from the changes implemented. In the United Kingdom for example, it has been realised that the redevelopment of ailing cities is a long-term task, requiring a 10-15-year strategic horizon, rather than the three-year project-based approach, which was the norm in the mid-1990s (Carley, 2000). Extending the horizon may also help to strengthen the entrepreneurialist model, which in general tends to prioritise short-term results and sometimes suffers from market myopia.

In that context, the UK government has prepared the way for new regional spatial and urban (e.g., core cities) strategies and developed informative long-term analysis. The government attaches importance to maximising the strength of the economic context contained in the existing framework of planning guidance and releasing the national economic potential of provincial city regions. Metropolitan planning should increasingly target the creation of new knowledge and deliver policy goals on a broader economic, social and environmental scale and within an appropriate time frame.[3] Creativity and innovation are strengthened when these functions are located close together. Spatial policies which prioritise higher densities for urban core development will directly support the growth of knowledge assets and the higher-value economic functions that these attract.

In France, the long-term character of planning is widely recognised. The articulation between strategic plans and planning instruments has been considerably reinforced in the last two to three years. This has been facilitated by the strong involvement of the central state in the territorial policy process, and by the growing recognition of planning as a policy tool for regional competitiveness policy. Several strategic plans should now be available at the regional level,[4] reflecting central government, regional council and city views.

2.1.2. Broadening planning goals

In strategic spatial planning, it is now acknowledged that individual policies could have adverse consequences, thus emphasising the necessity to develop integrated or holistic views. The integration in the planning agenda of new goals such as sustainability is nevertheless not an easy task. Sustainability and sustainability policies are widely understood to recognise the coexistence of the economic, the social and the environmental spheres in the city. It is not entirely understood, however, that sustainability is not the result of a simple sum of traditional policies addressed to economic, social and environmental goals. The outcomes of such policies could conflict with one another, if the three different goals are not taken into consideration simultaneously and from the beginning. On the other hand, policy tools typical of the three fields may enhance each other's effect if implemented in an integrated way. To that end, regulatory principles, such as allocative efficiency (internalisation of social costs), distributive efficiency and environmental equity (inter- and intra-generation) should be applied, but such measures could increase the burden of stakeholders and restrict their margin of maneuver (Camagni, 2000).

In this context, strategic planning is facing different options. In certain countries, sustainable urban development has often converged on the ideal of the compact city. In other countries, the green city has been advocated. These two models have different implications. "Whereas the compact city model implies that future needs for development should be met through densification, present understanding of the consequences of the green city model indicates that new development should rather take place as spatial extension of the city." Energy-conscious spatial planning points clearly in the direction of relatively dense patterns (inner-city residents travel considerably less by car than their outer-area counterparts) (Naess, 2001). A high utilisation of built-up areas is also favorable to lower needs for space-heating. However, high density conflicts with the desire of residents for green areas close to home. In many cases, planners seem to take for granted that the goal of sustainability is largely consistent with the prevailing lifestyle and consumption habits in the cities. The reduction of environmentally-harmful activities might also be difficult to achieve in the context of both the entrepreneurial and incrementalist models.

Whatever their inclination, member countries' spatial policies are increasingly underpinned by the sustainable development paradigm, with the idea being to promote an integrative approach.[5] This could be achieved by applying special types of regulation with regard to air, water quality and waste; policies might prioritise balanced considerations with regard to place quality, be relatively restrictive in accommodating road-based transport and attempt to reduce urban expansion, encouraging sprawl at the cost of sustainable assets. Protective zoning might also be used to secure environment conservation. In several countries, legislation has been introduced to require local authorities to carry out impact analyses, as well as subsequent monitoring of their strategic-level plans. In some of them, the findings of these analyses are made public, thus ensuring a higher degree of transparency and accountability.

An example of a sustainability-based framework is the European Spatial Development Perspective (ESDP), a programme completed and endorsed by European Member States' Ministers in 1999. ESDP, with its central concern of economic competitiveness, social cohesion and environmental sustainability, notably emphasises sustainable development, prudent management and the protection of the natural and cultural heritage.[6] It pinpoints the need to relieve transport systems through appropriate planning and spatial development policy by enhancing intermodal transport chains and strengthening environmentally-friendly transport systems. Natural and cultural heritage are considered as main assets that often need protection. They not only serve cultural development, but also, more generally, city and regional economic development through creative management. This framework was instrumental in influencing spatial planning, notably in many cross-border and peripheral areas in the EU (*e.g.*, in Northern Ireland and the Irish Republic) (Murray, 2004).

Achieving sustainability is a challenge for the entrepreneurialist planning mode, and even a dilemma. Consensus across all stakeholder groups may be difficult to arrive at and tensions could emerge. It could be considered by some corporate interests to be unfavorable to the business climate. Rigid regulatory frameworks would be harmful for developer investment and public-private partnerships. Alliance-building could, nevertheless, help to clarify dialogue and negotiation. Open and well-informed planning would certainly contribute to the emergence of common strategies for ecological sustainability and the identification of win-win solutions. Indeed, what is expected from urban strategic planning is not a conflict-free city, but one that knows how to manage its conflict.

2.1.3. *Adjusting to metropolitan areas*

Strategic planning is also more coherent when it corresponds to functional regions. While the record has been very uneven for major cities, the attempt to do so has been particularly marked in the most dynamic urban areas. In the case of Barcelona, strategic planning has increasingly looked at wider scales than the city itself. Its entrepreneurial agenda has pushed for more comprehensive plans. The most recent (2002) is considered a success and an example for the counties in the region. In Paris, there are a number of plans established at city and regional level, and recently, the mayor has started a dialogue with the municipalities in the immediate vicinity of the capital.

In general, given the different approaches, as well as the diversity of commitment and policy emphasis of urban authorities, city and metropolitan plans are highly variable in terms of their comprehensiveness and insightfulness. The strategic content of these plans could be limited or relatively narrowly defined, sometimes only providing a vision for the future that embraces a number of general objectives or core values of the city. It involves planning and anticipating trends, but could lack data and quantification, as well as mechanisms for evaluating the results.

3. Collaborative planning and network-based urban governance

To address these difficulties, urban planning systems are increasingly evolving into a more network-based and flexible structure with closer collaboration between levels of government and the integration of many stakeholders in the wake of the decentralisation trend prevailing in a number of countries. The new emphasis on co-operation involves constructing new policy relationships for strategy development and integrating new actors in the planning exercise in a multi-governance environment, i.e., not only public bodies, but also coalitions of local interests, including private investors, business associations, property developers and the community of voluntary and non-governmental organisations. In many areas, the increasing focus on large projects and the development of particular districts have given the business sector a driving role in planning.

3.1. The rise in partnerships

Traditionally, spatial development plans were produced by technical teams in interaction with key politicians. Hierarchical relations between levels of government were the only mode of management. This was reflected in master plans produced by experts and public investment involvement. Public sector emphasis was focused on regulating the private sector and imposing a rigid pattern on land use and development, incompatible with the changing nature of the economy.

National urban strategies are now further elaborated at the regional and city level to deliver more competitiveness-oriented strategies. The tendency towards fiscal and financial decentralisation in many countries has increased the accountability of municipalities and their willingness to embark on urban development projects. As a consequence, an increasing sense of entrepreneurialism has been exhibited by both public and private actors. Non-profit agencies producing amenities (*e.g.*, schools, hospitals, public transportation agencies) have also changed their attitudes, while becoming less dependent on central subsidies.

The key element in emerging approaches relates to partnerships. The current interest in stakeholder politics and "joined-up thinking" suggests that partnerships may be an effective remedy to the failings of policies developed with insufficient communication between different organisations and agencies. Partnerships are also a necessity for local governments that can't meet the scale of problems they face.

There is currently a great deal of experimentation underway in collaborative strategy making. Some of these efforts emphasise joint strategy-making between groups of municipalities. Some collaborative efforts arise through formalised partnerships or mechanisms for formal arrangements between partners to pursue joint interests. Such arrangements underpinned the strategy for the Stockholm region, where complex problems need to be addressed. In Italy, formal mechanisms have been used in some multi-municipal partnerships (*e.g.*, territorial pacts). In Belgium, the Brussels regional government established semi-official bodies (*e.g.*, the Brussels Development Society) and estate agencies to better operate in the private market. In Spain, the consortium formula has been used in Madrid in the development of new urban land, by giving landowners permission to build in some areas at market price, in exchange for urbanised land for social housing. These partnerships have produced a considerable increase in building infrastructure.

3.2. The role of local planning

In that context, local governments are expected to play a crucial role. Local governments have the best knowledge of local assets and spatial demand and, consequently, are the most able to develop innovation capabilities and encourage better utilisation of spatial opportunities. The local context is, in particular, well-placed to integrate the different stakeholder approaches into a coherent and growth-enhancing socio-spatial conception and avoid some of the negative consequences of individual policies. Furthermore, in many countries, central authorities have no desire to be involved in all planning matters and are increasingly decentralising responsibilities to sub-national tiers of government.

Greater latitude given to local governments allows for the diversity of local situations to be reflected in local and urban plans. More freedom for municipalities could encourage local planners, developers and firms to actively work together in developing metropolitan and urban regional plans. In the case of Seoul, decentralisation reforms allowed the city government to increasingly plan some large programmes for urban regeneration and city development. Recourse to PPP has intensified (in 2004, a total of 114 projects were entrusted to the private sector by the city). In Barcelona, the plans have all been promoted by the municipalities, the county being relatively inactive.

Other advantages could be derived from new institutional forms and channels of communication. Local planners could act as mediators and catalysts in a multi-actor environment and use to the fullest their strategic knowledge and local expertise. However, there has also been criticism of an often "closed" and "corporatist" approach, with less public accountability. Local planners are said to be accustomed to bureaucratic approaches and hierarchical behavior, hence slowing down their responsiveness to private sector demands.

3.3. Networks in a fragmented environment

The involvement of the private sector is essential within the entrepreneurialist approach, as this ensures that public policy makers are well informed about the needs of business and can, in turn, mobilise firms behind the strategic plan. Networks are being established in member countries through the engagement not only of municipalities and local agencies, but also through the involvement of business associations, firms and other private-sector groups. These networks function through consultation, listening or consensus-building. It is the reason why public policy literature talks about governance of a region rather than government of urban regions. This extension of spatial policies to a large network of stakeholders does not necessitate that these actors have a formal status.

Chambers of commerce and trade associations help provide a level playing-field. It is important that these entities acquire the capacity to articulate interests at the metro-regional level and not only at the city or suburb level. When associations represent the interests of both large and small firms, it is necessary that the latter interest could be fairly represented. In certain countries, delivery of public policies requires the participation of the private sector (*e.g.*, in the United Kingdom, the RDA or in the Netherlands for most multi-purpose agencies). Many informal co-operative structures in the regions also include leading economic actors.

Institutional fragmentation at the local level is common in many metropolitan cities and can be a brake on collaborative planning, making co-operation with the private sector more complex. When planning and administrative functions are divided between several local authorities, concerns about localism are important, as well as local governments increasingly inclined to compete with each other. Obstacles to planning networks depend on structural problems (see Box 4.1) or on the specific configuration of metropolitan organisations. The following examples illustrate the difficulty of finding suitable arrangements and the emergence of tradeoffs between the different planning scales in some contexts:

- *Lack of unified metropolitan government*: In Barcelona, the city experimented with a unique structure: the Metropolitan Corporation of Barcelona (CMB), created in 1974, in charge of approving urban planning and providing services. Considerable impetus was given to planning projects, in particular during the period 1979-1985, and the CMB was subsequently endowed with a significant budget. But the corporation was abolished by decision of the regional government in 1987. Services are now co-ordinated by two entities and responsibility for planning has reverted to the region. Thus, the negotiating capacity of the metropolitan entities has presumably been weakened and co-ordination could have been made more difficult. Debate is ongoing between the Catalan government and the city government on how to achieve joint management of the various domains (through a charter) (Kreukels, *et al.*, 2002).

> **Box 4.1. Co-ordination across jurisdictions**
>
> Urban plans span not only local government boundaries but often two or more administrative regions, as well. This poses major problems for co-ordination in general and makes planning and the implementation more complex. Manifestations of poor co-ordination include:
>
> - Poor quality of public services where administrative boundaries inhibit efficient use of resources and investment;
> - Duplication and waste where sectoral policies, often managed by different levels of government, are poorly integrated and have different, even contradictory objectives;
> - Reluctance to share resources and information among sub-national authorities;
> - Dispersal of funds to a multiplicity of agencies that have similar mandates.
>
> Many problems of co-ordination are related directly to weaknesses in the system of governance, which often does not adequately reward co-operative behavior. There is a tendency to view public investment in infrastructure and service provision at regional or local levels as being spatially neutral, i.e., as following an optimal economic allocation model; whereas, in fact, the process is strongly influenced by spatial factors, in particular local political dynamics. The choice of what type of infrastructure is funded or where a particular facility is located will have both an economic and political bottom line, and the ability of a governance system to arbitrate competing demands, across, as well as within, administrative borders, goes a long way to explaining the effectiveness of policy implementation.
>
> Spatial planning is one means by which these different interests can be mediated into a coherent strategy. However, planning instruments are often based on administrative boundaries, and it is only recently that cross-jurisdictional planning instruments have become more common.

- *Specific problems of polycentric structure*: The competitiveness of polycentric regions is dependent on the quality of intraregional connectivity and public transport. In the absence of strong leadership, co-ordinating urban planning and economic strategy is an arduous task with no evident solution. The Randstadt area (conceived in 1958 as a would-be Dutch world city) has no dominant center and still remains a potential metropolis after 50 years, having failed to become functional. The national government and the platform (Regio Randstadt) have divergent views regarding what to do about this situation. The former wants to designate the region as a network; the latter insists that there is a need to reinforce the links between the poles because they have not yet reached critical mass.[7]

- *Risk of weakening planning issues:* In Dublin, the centralisation of strategies has remained strong and the move towards entrepreneurialism has resulted in the marginalisation of local planning functions and the undermining of planning powers through the establishment of special-purpose renewal agencies. "Local government planning functions have been bypassed and, to a large extent, replaced by often-centralised quasi-private agencies. Local planners have often sought refuge in integrated micro-area planning." In addition, the deepening entrepreneurial orientation of urban governance has tended to refocus planning functions towards short-term operation (McGuirk, 2001) Given the lack of resources of the Dublin Regional Authority and its limited power, increasing focus on the micro-area could lead to downplaying strategic planning issues and metroscale development.

On the other hand, it is sometimes argued that frustrations of fragmentation might force stakeholders to look for consensus-building processes and encourage a shift to multi-governance and co-operation.

Despite these fragmentation problems, many (unitary) countries are devolving a new role to sub-national levels of government in order to foster innovation and reinforce subsidiary. The Netherlands, for example, has an explicit policy in this field. In a new policy memorandum (2006), an integrated document produced by four different Dutch ministries,[8] the government underlines its new approach to government control, which might be summarised by the injunction: "centralise if necessary, decentralise if possible" (Van der Burg, 2006). It involves, moreover, a systematic redistribution of planning tasks. Local and regional governments are formally invited to participate in spatial planning in order to arrive at local and regional visions. Public authorities will have to take on the role of partners to enterprising individuals and companies, reinforcing the dynamic, rather than working against it with a complex system of rules. An important aim of the new policy is to set in motion dynamism in spatial processes and to avoid imposing specific requirements on spatial development unless national and international interests are at stake.

Several governments have also tried to better align strategic thinking and planning implementation at the local level, and to alleviate the regulatory burden and its formalism. In France, this has been emphasised in a new piece of legislation adopted in 2000 (the so-called SRU law), the objective of which being to reform the planning toolkit. The main innovation is to create a new urban document which will reflect the strategic approach of local authorities (sustainable development plan, or PAAD) and will be a prerequisite for the elaboration of the new local plan (PLU)-see Box 4.2. The goal is to change the philosophy, no longer giving priority to the individual property-owner, but rather to collective development projects.

Box 4.2. **The *Plan Local d'Urbanisme* in France (PLU) and the *Schéma de Cohérence Territorial* (SCOT)**

The PLU replaces the former Land Use Plans (POS) that were initiated by the 1967 land orientation law. It aims at taking into account the changes in the urban landscape, the emergence of local government powers, the growing number of conflicts over the use of land and the increasing importance of environmental issues. PLUs are designed for a 10-15-year period and are appropriate mostly for urban municipalities (about 18 000 of them). So far, about 2000 (generally the most dynamic cities) have adopted a PLU (the new legislation was passed in 2000). In order to give adequate time to the municipalities to elaborate a plan, a transition period has been organised (POS/PLU) and a simplified procedure for the revision introduced. When an agglomeration (a co-operative structure of urban municipalities, *i.e.*, a kind of functional urban region) has been created, the PLU is designed at this level. The main strategic tool is the PAAD (*Projet d'aménagement et de développement durable*) which is elaborated in concertation with stakeholders, elected officials, local politicians and sometimes the public. The new system obviously represents a step away from the dirigist policy that prevailed in the past.

Another initiative has been to instruct sub-national governments to build up special schemes called SCOT (*Schéma de cohérence territorial*). They are elaborated by group of municipalities within a functional area and, in particular, urban areas, *i.e.*, covering city centres and the periphery. The city plan (PLU), local urban transport plan and housing plan need to be compatible with the SCOT to be valid and enforced. This document sets the main orientations of a group of adjacent communities (*intercommunalité*) for a ten-year period. It should ensure a balance between urban renewal and the rural periphery, preserve the diversity of urban functions and social mix and achieve competitive and sustainable development.

In the case of the Paris region, a PLU (2005-2020) has recently been established for the city. It is said to be pro-enterprise and pro-employment. Geographic Sector 1, where employment is a priority, has been extended, as well as the incubator and university campus areas. The development of "smart" offices is also encouraged in Sector 2, mainly targeting residential development. A balance is maintained all over the city between services to people and high value-added services, notably through maintaining an appropriate share of low-cost housing. Housing remains a big issue given the need to slow down the gentrification process and to maintain a social mix in the city.

A number of SCOTs are being studied in the region, but none of them has proven itself yet. The City of Paris is not involved in any SCOT.

3.4. Vertical co-ordination and regional levels

Efficient policy delivery also implies some type of articulation between the different levels of government to avoid or limit divergent planning approaches (see Box 4.3) and encourage vertical collaboration. While countries exhibit different systems of governance, the regional or medium level seems to play a pivotal role in most of them, given the relevance of the functional area and the growing economic significance of the city-region dimension. This strengthening of the medium level reflects a trend towards optimality and/or decisions from the central government.

- In the United States, the responsibility for land-use planning is exerted by the states according to the constitution, but practically it is delegated to the municipalities. In the 1970s, in view of the public preoccupation with the impacts of sprawl on the environment and agricultural activities, a number of states reassumed roles in spatial planning. A number of municipalities in large metropolitan areas adopted local growth systems that often reduce density. Accelerating urban sprawl and its consequences: reduced open space and recreational area, increased traffic congestion on suburban arteries and highways, pollution, etc., have created new concerns. Thirteen states (of 50) have adopted new or strengthened incentive-based growth management systems.

- In the United Kingdom, following the work on the city-region concept, the government has put an increasing focus on regional competitiveness and on the links between cities and their hinterland.[9] The main purpose of the new regional planning guidance (RPG), incorporating regional transport strategy, is to provide a strategy within which local authority development plans and local transport plans can be prepared. This RPG should also provide the longer-term planning framework for the Regional Development Agencies' (RDA) economic strategies. In Birmingham, for example, the regional planning body has redirected and rebalanced its spatial strategy. It was recognised that a change was needed to better co-ordinate economic, environmental, education, health and transport policies. Nonetheless, government planning policy guidance is sometimes criticised for being ambiguous and abstract.

In some countries there are, nevertheless, few rules that require harmonisation of local plans with overarching general policy, thus leaving local governments with considerable latitude to design plans. In those cases, it seems that often planning practices fill the gap. In Stockholm, for example, the (metropolitan) county council produces a combined regional land use and transportation plan. The plan suggests principles for the use of land and water, as well as guidelines for the location of development and infrastructure, but does not have the force of law. These plans are optional but "they represent a

Box 4.3. **The different levels of planning**

The highest level of plan is the macro-level plan – usually at the national level but also in some countries at the large region level. At this level, the use and nature of spatial plans varies considerably. Some countries, for example the United Kingdom and the United States, have no national spatial development plan as such. Others are mainly conceptual (*e.g.*, France or Japan), concerned with economic development issues in the aggregate, but not with allocative or land use decisions directly.

Despite some variations, the planning systems of OECD countries can, in general, be said to encompass the following fundamental functions:

- Spatial planning provides a long- or medium-term spatial strategy in pursuit of agreed objectives (often controlling regional disparities and working towards sustainable development).
- Spatial planning is also frequently a tool to co-ordinate various sectoral policies in pursuit of these spatial development objectives.
- Spatial planning is increasingly understood as a mechanism of co-ordination and interaction which enables sub-national governments to shape their own spatial development policies in conformity with national or even international policy goals, and facilitates regional and local adaptations of national policies.

At the middle level, corresponding to an administrative region and especially to an urban region, plans combine both the land use planning aspects of the micro-level plans and some type of strategic approach. In many countries, they cover a number of jurisdictions, though in most cases the lowest-level unit (*e.g.*, the municipality) retains legal control of land use and zoning. As such, middle level plans are often illustrative of efforts to build more innovative horizontal governance mechanisms. It is at this level that spatial plans are most directly concerned with major physical development (at a scale that has regional or even national impact, but that also depends on an awareness of land use issues).

Micro- or sub-regional level plans are the basis for the spatial planning system in the sense that they show what types of land use are permitted for each zone or parcel of land where basic infrastructure (*e.g.*, roads, railways, drains, etc.) is located, and what rights are associated with each parcel of land (*e.g.*, rights of way, style of construction, billboards and signs, etc.). It is at this level that spatial planning is most directly concerned with land use and, to a large degree, the enforcement of planning decisions taken at higher levels.

consensus between the municipalities and long-term development goals". It is important to notice that plans and strategies for economic and social development have been introduced by the county council as well, without being requested by the central government to do so. These trends, however, have not resulted in more intense collaboration with the private sector (Kreukels, et al., 2002). In general, planners rely on land use planning and new infrastructure to spur private investment rather than involving business representatives directly in planning negotiations.

3.5. Process and implementation

In the collaborative approach emerging and expanding as stressed above, there are conflicts to be addressed. Some of these cannot be solved by consensus-building processes and will remain to be settled by political or legal decisions. This means that careful attention is needed to exactly how a strategy development process moves through its various stages: opening up the issues, consolidating them, developing strategic concepts and dealing with outstanding conflicts. A helpful idea is the idea of forums, arenas and courts (Bryson and Crosby). Forums can help meet the need for more informal ways of collaborating to identify issues and develop approaches to understanding urban and regional dynamics. Arenas are more-structured situations where strategic frameworks are developed and selected in ways that maximise shared-ownership. Courts provide a necessary complement to collaborative processes, in recognition of the potential that some conflicts will remain unsolved (Bryson and Crosby, 1992; Healey, 1998).

These forums and arenas could be organised to generate contracts between stakeholders. Such contractual arrangements have been developed by a number of governments to reach agreements, mainly between the different tiers of government. Although not always designed specifically for planning purposes, these contracts have the advantage of making formal links between actions governed by spatial plans and implementation by lower levels, often governed in turn by more local planning instruments. The use of contracts provides, at least in theory, a clearer mechanism by which to link different-scale plans and reinforce the role of planning instruments in assigning responsibilities among government actors, co-ordinating policy implementation and monitoring the coherence of policy implementation across sectors and across levels of government.

More generally, assessment of the planning exercise and of its impact provides a means to improve partnership processes and to favor the continuous adaptation of the entrepreneurship approach. Although a tradition in the private sector, evaluation procedures do not seem to have been extensively used in metropolitan and city planning activities to date.[10] Relatively few countries have acquired an evaluation culture in spatial planning. Traditionally, planning systems are poor at measuring their impact on development patterns against targets and indicators. Impact analyses are considered difficult to use because they tend to be medium- and long-term endeavors. Criteria to evaluate the effectiveness of spatial planning are mostly sectoral, at least when it comes to short term evaluations (*e.g.*, concerning regional economic development, transport and communications). These evaluations are mostly process-oriented, while their effectiveness can only be assessed after some years. Performance measurement is further complicated by the fact that planning systems are only one among many influences on regional development.

Conclusions: challenges and future perspectives

In the last decade, the entrepreneurial model has established itself in member countries' planning activities as a main reference. The new planning philosophy puts stress on market-based approaches, vision-building and integration of socio-economic and environment-preservation goals. One of its important aims is to use business sector instruments to increase efficiency and develop a more project-friendly environment.

Strategic planning, which emerged from the practice of large corporations, has become a main tool for government to integrate competitiveness concerns in spatial strategies. Its extension to the sub-national levels including cities and metropolises has been reinforced in a majority of countries by a general move towards decentralisation of policies and granting more responsibility to lower tiers of government, according to the subsidiarity principle. Cities have gained more margin for maneuver, while city-region linkages were emphasised. As regional and city councils are closer to citizens, central governments are paving the way for different regional and local approaches and policy interpretations. But, basic standards need to be adhered to.

Another feature of the new planning model is a more pluralistic approach by public authorities, based on public-private partnerships. The pressure for more collaborative processes, involving a much wider range of interests, has increased. Previously, planning was in the hands of public agencies working for the construction of the welfare state, and therefore mainly orientated towards the delivery of social services. It is clear that an important prerequisite to augment city competitiveness is to better exploit the knowledge, innovative capacities and commitment of a greater number of urban actors.

While the entrepreneurial approach has been highly successful in increasing public and private investment in major cities, for example in southern Europe and the United Kingdom, it carries with it a number of internal tensions and sometimes pitfalls. This can lead to situations that hamper decision making and provide unsustainable planning solutions. First, a deepening entrepreneurial orientation of urban governance in a city could refocus planning functions towards short-term facilitative operations undertaken in the name of place competitiveness. Short-term initiatives can be useful to focus resources and human energy but they may run some risk. An opportunistic outlook to attract private sector development might result, for example, in a lack of coherence between land use and the offer of transport services, underprovision in public space and poor aesthetic quality of many of the buildings (Brownhill, 1990). Much depends here on the comprehensiveness of the metropolitan planning strategy and the extent to which it imposes itself on planners.

Second, in many countries, local government administration structures and boundaries have changed over the last period, often to take into account the geographical extension of cities (and also the move towards a polycentric pattern) and to reflect the new decentralisation ideal, but they seem to also favor lobbying and special interest groups. In some cases (mainly in unitary countries), the central government has maintained competitive bidding around government policy themes for local public spending. New forms of governance have emerged based on a polynodal character, with administrative/business relations often built around sectoral issues. While these interest groups might be given privileged status, they could encounter legitimacy problems, while antagonising others (Hull, 1998).

In other cases, growing fragmentation has affected cities in which administrative and planning functions are divided between several local authorities, often competing to attract lucrative investment – in terms of property tax (*e.g.*, retailing and office functions). This threatens the coherence of planning and the need to promote collective interest. Some governments have recentralised some planning functions to facilitate the development of large projects and to avoid such bias, the emergence of endless conflicts and prevent the waste of public money.

Third, these reorganisations in local administration (usually in unitary countries) raise the question of "whether the debate about spatial issues in urban areas is now located within actual development plan-making arenas with key stakeholders interacting. Or whether the philosophy of debates generated outside, on positioning in the global market and ensuring comparative advantage, will be transferred into the plan" (Hull, 1998). In the same vein, it may be asked whether the citizens concerned identify with the main choices and whether they can play a role in the decision-making process. Without real public participation, the entrepreneurial approach loses its legitimacy and remains a confluence of business and local interests subjected to electoral cycles and evolving local leadership.

The extent to which these issues will be addressed and policy solutions brought about will have a significant impact on the consolidation of the entrepreneurial model. Its future will probably also depend on the upgrading of the knowledge and the training of local administrations. In many places, there is a need to strengthen local planners' expertise and to adopt a new organisational culture less influenced than in the past by bureaucratic procedures and more conducive to rapid decision-making processes and flexible attitudes. This means not only that local governments have to make an extra investment in knowledge and skills, but also that national governments will have to design a knowledge roadmap and disseminate it to the city and local levels.

Notes

1. The above short developments are extracted from the chapters on Barcelona, London and Vienna in *Metropolitan Governance and Spatial Planning* by A. Kreukels, W. Salet and A. Thornley.
2. These (mega-) trends include: the emergence of the knowledge economy, the role of metropolis as an engine for innovation, the consolidation of the service sector or the growing importance of education assets and cultural amenities in the global competition of cities.
3. The term "ideopolis" has been coined to express this concept.
4. Three types of strategic documents have been elaborated at the regional level: the PASER (*Projet d'action strategique de l'Etat en region*) designed by the Prefet, the SRADT (*Schéma régional d'aménagement du territoire*), a more long-term plan and the SRDE (*Schéma régional de développement économique*) by the Regional Council. Within the framework of the city and agglomeration contracts other documents, called city or agglomeration projects, are also necessary.
5. For example, in the case of London, it consists in accommodating growth through the development of opportunity areas and areas for intensification and inducing regeneration in areas suffering from social exclusion and economic deprivation. Cross-cutting themes include the need to co-ordinate transport and development in order to develop public transport and tackle congestion problems. See the "London Plan: A Summary", February 2004.
6. Overarching spatial development principles include, apart from the wise management of the natural and cultural heritage, the development of a balanced and polycentric urban system and parity of access to infrastructure and knowledge.
7. The Ministries in charge see the Randstad area as a single urban network. They consider that the international competitive position of the region as a whole needs to be enhanced. At the same time, they nevertheless divide the area into three distinct economic core areas (Amsterdam: i.e., the North wing, Rotterdam/ the Hague: the South wing and the Utrecht region). The idea is that boosting the competitiveness of each of these areas will stimulate the whole of the Randstad. The intra-regional diversity of the area is seen as a key advantage in international competition. The regional platform opts for a partially different strategy, giving primacy to a Randstad-wide perspective. They consider that critical mass has not

been reached in each part, and prioritise a strengthening of the relationships between the different parts, with varying implications for planning, infrastructure-building and suburban development. See Lambregts (2005).

8. The National Spatial Strategy safeguards important values like nature, landscape and increases public safety while allowing space for development. This strategy sets out policy up to the year 2020. It is the pivotal policy product of the government. The Ministry for VROM has earmarked EUR 418 million from the Economy Structure Enhancing Fund to boost spatial quality projects.

9. It is recognised that cities boost regions by providing a critical mass of public and private knowledge institutions, strategic business services, connectivity, highly-paid jobs, a concentration of culture, leisure and sports and transport hubs. Conversely, cities rely on regions for space for economic and infrastructure projects, a wider range of urban and rural housing options, distinctive urban centres, a range of business sites and premises, a wider workforce, opportunities for countryside leisure and feedback on reputation and performance.

10. Some initiatives are nevertheless worth mentioning, since they are signs of a change in attitudes towards evaluation. In the United Kingdom, the government introduced a requirement for a sustainable development appraisal of the environmental, economic and social impacts of development options to inform and accompany draft Regional Planning Guidance. Several states in America, such as Oregon and New Jersey, have adopted benchmarking processes in which specific goals or benchmarks are established to monitor progress in achieving state goals over time. Benchmarks range from social indicators to environmental indicators (rate of land consumption) or economic indicators (employment growth). Since this benchmarking effort requires monitoring of dozens or even hundreds of obscure indicators, the tendency is now to move towards a dashboard approach. Under this approach a relatively small number of easily-obtainable, readily-understood benchmarks are utilised to show general trends and achievement.

ISBN 978-92-64-02240-9
OECD Territorial Review
Competitive Cities
A New Entrepreneurial Paradigm in Spatial Develompent
© OECD 2007

Chapter 5

Conclusion

This chapter draws lessons from past policy experiences analysed in the previous chapters, and identifies the pitfalls of "narrowness" in various forms in the entrepreneurial approaches so far, and discusses how they can be improved. The chapter also shows how the role of local governments should change by adapting to the new policy framework created by the new entrepreneurial paradigm.

5. CONCLUSION

The emergence of the competitiveness agenda as a dominant approach in urban policy planning has fundamentally altered the mode of urban governance from managerialism to entrepreneurialism, which is characterised by pro-active and pro-economic growth attitudes, public-private partnership, strategic approaches, and the adoption of the private sector's marketing methodology.

This shift towards urban entrepreneurialism opened up a new dimension in urban spatial development by bringing in various policy innovations. For example, it identified and exploited new potential in such policies as cultural policy and event-hosting for urban economic regeneration. It aims to harness the private sectors' power for urban spatial development, and exploit market potential to the fullest by introducing new modes of regulatory measures to stimulate private innovation and strengthen market functioning. It has created a flexible institutional framework, which marks a shift from government to governance in urban policy planning.

1. Pitfalls of "narrowness"

However, policy experience over the past decades has shown that challenges exist for entrepreneurialism to realise its full potential and prepare itself for the new policy context in the 21st century by overcoming various aspects of narrowness inherent in previous policy approaches employing urban entrepreneurialism.

1.1. Building unique assets

First, too much dependence on the part of planners on a handful of successful cases as "good practices" resulted in strong similarities among strategies and the built-environments created by them, which led to the loss of local distinctiveness and uniqueness. The problem is further aggravated by the objectives of urban regeneration that are often narrowly defined and simply focus on place promotion through physical renovation. Planners' efforts to appeal to stereotyped images of knowledge workers' tastes contributed to the creation of built environments that are strongly characterised by similarities in tastes and their consumption-oriented nature, which favours selected social groups with considerable disposable income (Brindley, et al., 1996).

Similarities have not only been evident in spatial development policy but also in promotional incentives offered to external investors. The adoption of similar templates for city promotion strategies by cities that engage in place competition would trigger the competition of "offering more of the same", which in turn would create a buyers' market and undermine the efficacy of such strategies that entail considerable financial burdens on taxpayers.

Urban entrepreneurialism has aimed at being creative in policy planning; however, the emergence of analogous cities and analogous strategies appears to suggest that the reinvention of urban entrepreneurialism is necessary to reconstruct future policy planning around the notion of identifying and building up unique local assets rather than focusing too much on image creation. Place promotion without unique local assets would fail to leave long-lasting effects on the local economy.

1.2. Avoiding short-termism

Building up unique local assets requires long-term policy efforts based on strategic vision. It cannot be obtained simply by short-term tactical thinking. However, short-termism arising from profit-maximising motives in entrepreneurial approaches creates the danger of precluding longer-term perspectives for city competitiveness. Similarly, excessive preoccupation with place marketing could override considerations for long-term policy measures to improve the economic fundamentals of the city. City marketing should go hand in hand with local capacity-building through education, job training and strengthening of indigenous industries.

Short-termism in entrepreneurial approaches would be particularly detrimental when it incurs the waste of resources indispensable for the capacity-building of future generations. For example, financial consequences brought about by failed projects for place marketing sometimes imposed long-lasting financial burdens on programmes for local capacity-building. The highly volatile nature of property markets would further heighten the risks involved. Policy planners should reflect soberly on what is at stake in adopting such high-risk strategies and where the balance should lie.

1.3. Holistic approach

Building up competitive advantages requires addressing a wide range of factors that determine the attractiveness of the local economy. Such holistic perspectives on city attractiveness are essential in spatial development policy, as well. It should not simply be directed towards physical attractiveness but also aim at enhancing social and environmental dimensions. Such efforts for economic competitiveness are intrinsically holistic.

Thus, spatial development policy is increasingly expected to address wider policy objectives; not only economic but also social, environmental and cultural policies are demanding policy planners' attention. What has become clear from past experience is that optimality in certain policy objectives does not necessarily correspond to optimality in others. Thus, strategies based on narrowly defined policy objectives would not result in the improvement of overall outcomes, with broader social, cultural and environmental objectives often residualised or diluted as they tend to be overridden by a centralised agenda of economic objectives (McGuirk and MacLaran, 2001).

Hence, urban entrepreneurialism should adopt more holistic approaches by incorporating wider policy objectives into coherent and complementary strategies. For example, market-led approaches, which have become the guiding principle due to their capacity to respond to rapid change, should aim at achieving wider policy goals by positively interacting with market forces, not simply by following them.

1.4. Learning process through wider participation

Public-private partnership provided a collaborative framework that is flexible and efficient. However, the narrowness of the scope of stakeholders that participate in the process has often made it difficult for residents to share the strategies coming out of such partnerships. The corporatist mode of decision making sometimes created the image that important decisions were made behind closed doors in an elitist circle to which ordinary citizens did not have proper access. The absence of effective means of securing accountability has been criticised as "the private management of public policy", and further made it difficult for citizens to share the entrepreneurial philosophy exercised in such processes.

Economic changes always have a wide range of preconditions, some of which may well be cultural and political. An entrepreneurial urban economy will only emerge through an active process of nurturing an entrepreneurial culture among residents. As Painter (1998) argues, all the actors in the local economy, including residents, business executives and government officials, have to learn how to be entrepreneurial.

However, thinking and behaving entrepreneurially, or competitively, is not something that actors know how to do automatically. To engender widespread entrepreneurialism among residents, it is essential that a learning experience takes place among all stakeholders. Indeed, one of the things most important to learn is how to participate (Painter, 1998). With different groups with different needs participating in governance arenas, it is clear that such a process makes high demands on the communication skills and willingness to co-operate of the actors involved. Learning to collaborate in such a "communicative and collaborative planning" process would develop a richer and more broadly-based understanding, through which collective approaches to resolving conflicts may emerge (Healey, 1995). Securing wider participation in the strategy planning process should provide such learning experience. As Deakin and Edwards (1993) argues, future urban entrepreneurialism should be supported by an institutional framework that represents such accountability, empowerment and partnership.

1.5. New role of local governments

The widened scope of participants will pose a challenge for local governments. There is a widespread concern about the efficacy of traditional local government structures and practices in planning in the face of the shift from government towards governance. To continue to play a central role, they need to develop new styles of operation which are amenable to contemporary modes of governance. This would require a departure from hierarchical and bureaucratically-determined practices that are driven by rules and regulations and which are slow to respond to new demands (McGuirk and MacLaran, 2001).

New modes of entrepreneurial urban governance would be increasingly structured by organisational forms involving negotiative networks stretching across governments, governmental agencies, private and third sectors, and there would be significant change in the mode and culture of interaction between them (McGuirk and MacLaran, 2001). In order to prepare for that change, local governments will need to operate in a more pluralist way than in the past, alongside a wide variety of public and private actors. It will be their task to stimulate and assist other actors to play their part, instead of, as well as, making provision themselves (Cochrane, 1991). In other words, the emphasis in the role of local governments would shift towards "enabling governments" from "providing governments". This creates a new emphasis on negotiation and network-building skills in the public sector (Brindley, et al., 1996).

These capacities would enable local government planners to mobilise effective networks which could work in an integrated fashion towards achieving broad environmental, economic, social and cultural planning aims. By strengthening such capacities, local governments would continue to play the central role in the process of policy making and implementation as mediators and catalysts, with their unique strategic overview together with local expertise and sensitivity to local interests. A strong and coherent leadership role played by local governments is crucial for urban entrepreneurialism to flourish in the fragmented structure of urban governance.

1.6. Final question: How entrepreneurial can urban entrepreneurialism continue to be?

With the irreversible trend of global economic integration, economic competitiveness will continue to occupy the central place in policy agenda, and entrepreneurialism will also continue to be a key feature in policy thinking. Indeed, the extent to which policy planning is entrepreneurial will be a crucial factor in determining city competitiveness. However, over the past years policy planners sometimes fell into a narrow definition of entrepreneurialism.

The essence of entrepreneurialism is to apply innovative thinking to policy planning in a strategic way, based on long-term vision. Such an attitude, which could be called "strategic innovativeness", is an essential property not only of competitive private enterprises in the global market, but also of competitive cities in ever-intensifying inter-city competition. Strategic innovativeness manifests itself in identifying and building up unique local assets, in harnessing "old policy tools" with totally new perspectives, and in mobilising the collective potential of all the actors in the local economy by motivating and empowering them.

The question that a policy planner employing an entrepreneurial approach should always ask himself/herself is just how entrepreneurial his/her approach is in this sense.

ISBN 978-92-64-02240-9
OECD Territorial Review
Competitive Cities
A New Entrepreneurial Paradigm in Spatial Develompent
© OECD 2007

Bibliography

Aaker, D. (1996), *Building Strong Brands*, The Free Press, New York.

Akerlof, George A. (1970), "The Market for 'Lemons': Quality Uncertainty and the Market Mechanism", *The Quarterly Journal of Economics*, Vol. 84, No. 3, pp. 488-500.

Albrechts, Louis (2001),"In Pursuit of New Approaches to Strategic Spatial Planning: a European Perspective", *International Planning Studies*.

Alexander, Don and Ray Tomalty (2002), "Smart Growth and Sustainable Development: Challenges, Solutions and Policy Directions", *Local Environment*, Vol. 7, No. 4, pp. 397-409.

Arnott, R. (1987), "Economic Theory and Housing", in E. S. Mills (ed.), *Handbook of Regional and Urban Economics*, Ch. 24, pp. 959-988.

Bailey, J. T. (1989), *Marketing Cities in the 1980s and Beyond*, American Economic Development Council, Chicago.

Barke, M. and K. Harrop (1994), "Selling the Industrial Town: Identity, Image and Illusion", in J. R. Gold and S. V. Wood (eds.), pp. 93-1114.

Barker, Kate (2004), "Review of Housing Supply: Securing Our Future Housing Needs, Final Report – Recommendations", HM Treasury, March, London.

Bennett, R. and S. Savani (2003), "The Rebranding of City Places: An International Comparative Investigation", *International Public Management Review*, Vol. 4, No. 2, pp. 70-87.

van den Berg, L., J. van der Meer and A. H. J. Otgar (1999), *The Attractive City: Catalyst for Economic Development and Social Revitalisation*, European Institute for Comparative Urban Research, Erasmus University, Rotterdam.

van den Berg, L., E. Braun and J. van der Meer (2004), *National Urban Policies in the European Union*, Euricur.

van der Burg, Arjen and Bart Vink (2006), "New Dutch Spatial Planning Policy Creates Space for Development", DISP 164, The Hague.

Best, Richard (1996), "Successes, Failures, and Prospects for Public Housing Policy in the United Kingdom", *Housing Policy Debate*, Vol. 7, Issue 3, Fannie Mae Foundation.

Boddy, T. (1992), "Underground and Overhead: Building the Analogous City", in M. Sorkin (ed.), *Variations on a Theme Park: The New American City and the End of Public Space*, Hill and Wang, New York, pp. 123-153.

Bock, S. (2006), "City 2030-21: Cities in Quest of the Future: New Forms of Urban and Regional Governance", *European Planning Studies*, April.

Boyer, M. C. (1992), "Cities for Sale: Merchandising History at South Street Seaport", in M. Sorkin (ed.), *Variations on a Theme Park: The New American City and the End of Public Space*, Hill and Wang, New York, pp. 123-153.

Bianchini, F. and M. Parkinson (eds.) (1993), *Cultural Policy and Urban Regeneration: The West European Experience*, Manchester University Press, Manchester.

Bogdon, A. S. and A. Can (1997), "Indicators of Local Housing Affordability: Comparative and Spatial Approaches", *Real Estate Economics*, Vol. 25, pp. 43-80.

Brindley, T., Y. Rydin and G. Stoker (1996), *Remaking Planning: The Politics of Urban Change*, Routledge, London.

Brown, Sarah and John G. Sessions (1997), "Housing, Privatization and the 'Right to Buy'", *Applied Economics*, Vol. 29, pp. 581-590.

Brownhill, S. (1990), *Developing London's Docklands: Another Great Planning Disaster?*, Paul Chapmann Publishing Ltd., London.

Burgess, J. (1981), "The Misunderstood City", *Landscapes*, Vol. 25.

Business Decision Ltd. (1974), "Industrial and Commercial Development: Summary of Research Findings".

Byrne, D. (2000), "Newcastle's Going for Growth: Governance and Planning in a Post-industrial Metropolis", *Northern Economic Review*, Vol. 30, pp. 3-16.

Camagni, Roberto (2000), "Policies for Spatial Development", DT/TDPC(2000)3, OECD, Paris.

Cameron, Stuart (2003), "Gentrification, Housing Redifferentiation and Urban Regeneration: 'Going for Growth' in Newcastle upon Tyne", *Urban Studies*, Vol. 40, No. 12, pp. 2367-2382.

Carley, M. (2000), "Urban Partnerships, Governance and the Regeneration of Britain's Cities", *International Planning Studies*, Vol. 5, No. 3.

Chatterton, P. and R. Unsworth (2004), "Making Space for Culture(s) in Boomtown: Some Alternative Futures for Development, Ownership and Participation in Leeds City Centre", *Local Economy*, Vol. 19, No. 4.

Chalkley, B. and S. Essex (1999), "Urban Development through Hosting International Events: A History of the Olympic Games", *Planning Perspectives*, Vol. 14, pp. 369-394.

CMHC (Canada Mortgage and Housing Corporation) (2000), "Research Report: International Experiences with Performance-Based Planning", Housing Affordability and Finance Series, CMHC.

Deakin, N. and J. Edwards (1993), *The Enterprise Culture and the Inner City*, Routledge, London.

DETR (1998), *Key Research on Easier Home Buying and Selling*.

Dieleman, Frans M. (1999), "The Impact of Housing Policy Changes on Housing Associations: Experiences in the Netherlands", *Housing Studies*, Vol. 14, No. 2, pp. 251-259.

Duncan, John (2005), "Performance-Based Building: Lessons from Implementation in New Zealand", *Building Research and Information*, March-April, Vol. 33, No. 2, pp. 120-127.

Eggers, Willian D. (1990), "Land Use Reform through Performance Zoning", *Policy Insight*, No. 120, Reason Foundation, Los Angeles.

Elsinga, Marja, Marietta Haffner, and Harry van der Heijden (2005), A Unitary Rental Market in Netherlands?: Theoretical Exploration and Empirical Evidence, paper presented at the ENHR conference "Housing in Europe – New Challenges and Innovations in Tomorrow's Cities", 29 June-3 July 2005, Reykjavik.

Fisher, P. S. and H. A. Peters (1996), "Taxes, Incentives and Competition for Investment", *The Region*, Vol. 10, pp. 52-57.

Florida, R. (2001), *The Geography of Bohemia*, Carnegie Mellon University, Pittsburg, PA.

Florida, R. (2002), *The Rise of the Creative Class: And how it's Transforming Work, Leisure, Community and Everyday Life*, Basic Books, New York.

Foliente, Greg C. (2000), "Developments in Performance-Based Building Codes and Standards", *Forest Products Journal*, July/August, Vol. 50, No. 7/8, pp. 12-21.

Friedrichs, J. and J. Dangschat (1993), "Hamburg: Culture and Urban Competition", in F. Bianchini and M. Parkinson (eds.), *Cultural Policy and Urban Regeneration: The West European Experience*, Manchester University Press, Manchester, pp. 114-134.

Freiden, Susan and Richard Winters (1997), "Performance Zoning Helps Key City's Comeback", *American City and County*, 1 June.

Fretter, A. D. (1993), "Place Marketing: A Local Authority Perspective", in G. Kearns and C. Philo (eds.), *Selling Places: The City as Cultural Capital, Past and Present*, Pergamon Press, Oxford, pp. 163-74.

Gann, David M., Yusi Wang and Richard Hawkins (1998), "Do Regulations Encourage Innovation?: The Case of Energy Efficiency in Housing", *Building Research and Information*, Vol. 26, No. 4, pp. 280-296.

Gold, J. (1980), *An Introduction to Behavioural Geography*, Oxford University Press, Oxford.

Goldberg, Victor P. (2002), "Economic Reasoning and the Framing of Contract Law: Sale of an Asset of Uncertain Value", in E. Brousseau and J.-M. Glachant (ed.), *The Economics of Contracts: Theories and Applications*, Cambridge University Press, Cambridge, UK.

Gordon, D. L. A. (1996), "Planning, Design and Managing Change in Urban Waterfront Redevelopment", *Town Planning Review*, Vol. 67, No. 3, pp. 261-90.

Gold, J. R. and S. V. Wood (eds.) (1994), *Place Promotion: The Use of Publicity and Marketing to Sell Towns and Regions*, John Wiley and Sons, Chichester.

Gómez, M. V. (1998), "Reflective Images: The Case of Urban Regeneration in Glasgow and Bilbao", *International Journal of Urban and Regional Research*, Vol. 22, No. 1, pp. 106-121.

Goodman, R. (1979), The Last Entrepreneurs, Boston.

Griffiths, R. (1993), "The Politics of Cultural Policy in Urban Regeneration Strategies", *Policy and Politics*, Vol. 21.

Griffiths, R. (1995), "Cultural Strategies and New Modes of Urban Intervention", *Cities*, Vol. 12, No. 4.

Gruis, Vincent, Nico Nieboer and Andrew Thomas (2004), "Strategic Asset Management in the Social Rented Sector: Approaches of Dutch and English Housing Associations", *Urban Studies*, Vol. 41, No. 7, pp. 1229-1248.

Hall, T. and P. Hubbard (eds.) (1998), *The Entrepreneurial City: Geographies of Politics of Regime and Representation*, Wiley, Chichester.

Hambleton, R. (1991), "The Regeneration of US and British Cities", *Local Government Studies*, September/October, pp. 53-69.

Harvey, D. (1988), "Voodoo Cities", *New Statesman and Society*, 30/9/88, pp. 33-35.

Harvey, D. (1989), "From Managerialism to Entrepreneurialism: The Transformation in Urban Governance in Late Capitalism", *Geografiska Annaler*, Vol. 71 B, No. 1, pp. 3-17.

HCEC (1988), "Third Report Session 1987-88: The Employment Effects of Urban Development Corporations", House of Commons Employment Committee, HMSO, London.

Healey, P. (1991), "Urban Regeneration and the Development Industry", *Regional Studies*, Vol. 25, No. 2, pp. 97-110.

Healey, P. (1995), "The Institutional Challenge for Sustainable Urban Regeneration", *Cities*, Vol. 12, No. 4, pp. 221-230.

Healey, P. (2004), "The Treatment of Space and Place in the New Strategic Spatial Planning in Europe", *International Journal of Urban and Regional Research*, March, Oxford.

Healey, P. (2006), "*Transforming Governance: Challenges of Institutional Adaptation and a New Politics of Space*", *European Planning Studies*, Vol. 14, No. 3.

Van der Heijden, Harry (2002), "Social Rented Housing in Western Europe: Developments and Expectations", *Urban Studies*, Vol. 39, No. 2, pp. 327-340.

Holocomb, B. (1994), "City Make-Overs: Marketing the Post-Industrial City", in J. R. Gold, and S. V. Ward (eds.), *Place Promotion: The Use of Publicity and Marketing to Sell Towns and Regions*, John Wiley and Sons, Chichester.

Home Office (1974), *Urban Programme Circular No. 11*, Home Office, London.

Hull, A. (1998), "The Development Plan as a Vehicle to Unlock Development Potential?" *Cities*, Vol. 15, No. 5, pp. 327, 335.

Imrie, R. and H. Thomas (1993), "The Limits of Property-Led Regeneration", *Environment and Planning C: Government and Policy*, Vol. 11, London.

IRCC (Inter-Jurisdiction Regulatory Collaboration Committee) (2000), *Performance-Based Codes Impact on International Trade*, IRCC.

Jacobs, B. (2000), *Strategy and Partnership in Cities and Regions: Economic Development and Urban Regeneration in Pittsburgh, Birmingham and Rotterdam*, Macmillan.

Japan Real Estate Trade Association (2002), "Survey on Consumers' Behaviour related to Real Estates Trade", on-line document.

Jones, A. (1998), "Issues in Waterfront Regeneration: More Sobering Thoughts – A UK Perspective", *Planning Practice and Research*, Vol. 13, No. 4.

Julier, G. (2005), "Urban Designscapes and the Production of Aesthetic Consent", *Urban Studies*, Vol. 42, pp. 5-6, 689-888.

Keil, A. (2006), "New Urban Governance Process on the Level of Neighbourhoods", *European Planning Studies*, Vol. 14, No. 3, pp. 299-320.

van Kempen, Ronald, and Hugo Priemus (1999), "Undivided Cities in the Netherlands: Present Situation and Political Rhetoric", *Housing Studies*, Vol. 14, No. 5, pp. 641-657.

Kotler, P., D. H. Haider and I. Rein (1993), *Marketing Places: Attracting Investment, Industry, and Tourism to Cities, States, and Nations*, Simon and Schuster.

Kreukels, A., W. Salet and A. Thornley (2002), *Metropolitan Governance and Spatial Planning: Comparative Case Studies of European City-Regions*, Spon Press, London.

Lambregts, B. (2005), *Polycentrism: Boon or Barrier to Metropolitan Competitiveness: The case of Randstadt*.

Law, C. M. (1993), *Urban Tourism: Attracting Visitors to Large Cities*, Mansell Publishing, London.

Leitner, H. and E. Sheppard (1998), "Economic Uncertainty, Inter-Urban Competition and the Efficacy of Entrepreneurialism", in T. Hall and P. Hubbard (eds.), *The Entrepreneurial City: Geographies of Politics of Regime and Representation*, Wiley, Chichester.

Loftman, P. and B. Nevin (1996), "Going for Growth: Prestige Projects In Three British Cities", *Urban Studies*, Vol. 33, pp. 991-1019.

Lovering, J. (1995), "Creating Discourses Rather Than Jobs" in P. Healey, S. Cameron, S. Davoudi, S. Graham and A. Madani-Pour (eds.), *Managing Cities: The New Urban Context*, John Wiley, Chichester.

McCarthy, J. (1998), "Reconstruction, Regeneration and Re-imaging: The Case of Rotterdam", *Cities*, Vol. 15, No. 5, pp. 337-344.

McCarthy, J. and S. H. A. Pollock (1997), "Urban Regeneration in Glasgow and Dundee: A Comparative Evaluation", *Land Use Policy*, Vol. 14, No. 2, pp. 137-149.

McGuirk, P. and A. McLaran (2001), "Changing Approaches to Urban Planning in an Entrepreneurial City: The Case of Dublin", *European Planning Studies*, Vol. 9, No. 4.

McGuirk, P., H. P. M. Winchester, and K. M. Dunn (1998), "On Losing the Local in Responding to Urban Decline: The Honeysuckle Redevelopment, New South Wales", in T. Hall and P. Hubbard (eds.), *The Entrepreneurial City: Geographies of Politics of Regime and Representation*, Wiley, Chichester.

McNeill, D. and A. While (2001), "The New Urban Economies", in R. Paddison (ed.), *Handbook of Urban Studies*, Sage, London.

Meacham, Brian J. (1998), *The Evolution of Performance-Based Codes and Fire Safety Design Methods*, NIST (National Institute of Standards and Technology, US Department of Commerce), Gaitherburg.

Meusen, Hans and Ronald van Kempen (1995), "Towards Residual Housing?: A Comparison of Britain and the Netherlands", *Netherlands Journal of Housing and the Built Environment*, Vol. 10, No. 3, pp. 239-258.

Mommaas, H. (2004), "Cultural Clusters and the Post-industrial City: Towards the Remapping of Urban Cultural Policy", *Urban Studies*, Vol. 41, No. 3.

Monclus, F.-J. (2003), "The Barcelona Model: An Original Formula? From Reconstruction to Strategic Urban Projects 1979-2004", *Planning Perspectives*, Oct.

Morris, M. H. and F. F. Jones (1999), "Entrepreneurship in Established Organizations: The Case of the Public Sector", *Entrepreneurship Theory and Practice*, Vol. 24/I, pp. 71-83.

Murray, Michael (2004), "Strategic Spatial Planning on the Island of Ireland: Towards a New Territorial Logic", Interdisciplinary Centre for Comparative Research in Social Sciences, Vienna.

Nakagawa, M. (2003), *Economic Analysis of Urban Housing Policy*, Nippon Hyoron Co., Tokyo.

Naess, P. (2001), "Urban Planning and Sustainable Development", *European Planning Studies*, Vol. 9, No. 4.

Nordic Council of Ministers (1998), *Housing Law in the Nordic Countries*, TemaNord, Copenhagen.

OECD (2005), "Policies to Enhance City Attractiveness: Outcome of the OECD International Symposium on City Attractiveness in Nagoya, Japan".

OECD (2006), *OECD Territorial Reviews: France*, OECD Publishing, Paris.

Paddison, R. (ed.) (2001), *Handbook of Urban Studies*, Sage.

Painter, J. (1998), "Entrepreneurs Are Made, Not Born: Learning and Urban Regimes in the Production of Entrepreneurial Cities", in T. Hall and P. Hubbard (eds.), *The Entrepreneurial City: Geographies of Politics of Regime and Representation*, Wiley, Chichester.

Parkinson, M., et al. (2004), Competitive European Cities: Where do the Core Cities Stand?, Office of the Deputy Prime Minister.

Patterson, M. (1999), "Re-appraising the Concept of Brand Image", *Journal of Brand Management*, Vol. 6, No. 6, pp. 409-426.

Pocock, D. and R. Hudson (1978), *Images of the Urban Environment*, Macmillan Press, London.

Priemus, Hugo and Frans Dieleman (1997), "Social Rented Housing: Recent Changes in Western Europe – Introduction", *Housing Studies*, Vol. 12, No. 4, pp. 421-425.

Priemus, Hugo (1998), "Redifferentiation of the Urban Housing Stock in the Netherlands: A Strategy to Prevent Spatial Segregation?", *Housing Studies*, Vol. 13, No. 3, pp. 301-310.

Quercia, Roberto G. and George C. Galster (1997), "Threshold Effects and the Expected Benefits of Attracting Middle-Income Households to the Central City", *Housing Policy Debate*, Vol. 8, Issue 2, Fannie Mae Foundation.

Richards, G. and J. Wilson (2004), "The Impact of Cultural Events on City Image: Rotterdam, Cultural Capital of Europe 2001", *Urban Studies*, Vol. 41, No. 10, pp. 1931-1951.

Roberts, P. and H. Sykes (eds.) (2000), *Urban Regeneration: A Handbook*, Sage.

Rodríguez, A., E. Martínez and G. Guenaga (2001), "Uneven Redevelopment: New Urban Policies and Socio-Spatial Fragmentation in Metropolitan Bilbao", *European Urban and Regional Studies*, Vol. 8, No. 2, pp. 161-178.

Rutheiser, C. (1996), Imagineering Atlanta: The Politics of Place in the City of Dreams, Verso, London.

Savitch, H. V. and P. Kantor (1995), "City Business: An International Perspective on Market Place Politics", *International Journal of Urban and Regional Studies*, Vol. 19, pp. 495-512.

Scottish Executive (2002), *Issues in Improving Quality in Private Housing: The First Report of the Housing Improvement Task Force*, Scottish Executive, Edinburgh.

Sewel, J., F. Twine and N. Williams (1984), "The Sale of Council Houses: Some Empirical Evidence", *Urban Studies*, Vol. 21, pp. 439-450.

Short, J. (1989), *The Humane City: Cities as if People Matter*, Blackwell, Oxford.

Skrodzki, B. (1989), "Urban Development and Culture in the Ruhn: the Views of Managers and Entrepreneurs", in V. Behr, F. Gnad and K. R. Kunzmann (eds.), *Culture, Economy and Development*, Dortmunder Beiträge zur Raumplanung, Vol. 51, IRPUD, Dortmund.

Social and Cultural Planning Office of the Netherlands (2000), "Social and Cultural Report 2000: The Netherlands in a European Perspective", Social and Cultural Planning Office of the Netherlands.

Sorkin, M. (ed.) (1992), *Variations on a Theme Park: The New American City and the End of Public Space*, Hill and Wang, New York.

Stone, C. N. (1989), *Regime Politics: Governing Atlanta 1946–1988*, University of Kansas Press, Lawrence, Kan.

Tomalty, R., A. Hercz and P. Spurr (2000), *Municipal Planning for Affordable Housing*, Canada Mortgage and Housing Corporation, Ottawa.

Torisu, E. (1986), *The Impact of a New Town Programme on Local Entrepreneurs: A Case Study of Peterborough*, M. Phil. Thesis, Department of Land Economy, University of Cambridge.

Turok, I. (1992) "Property-led Urban Regeneration: Panacea Or Placebo?", *Environment and Planning A*, Vol. 24, London.

UK ODPM (Office of the Deputy Prime Minister) (1999), *101 Home Buying and Selling in Denmark and New South Wales*, UK Office of the Deputy Prime Minister, London.

UK ODPM (2003a), *Housing Bill – Consultation on Draft Legislation*, UK Office of the Deputy Prime Minister, London.

UK ODPM (2003b), *Housing, Planning, Local Government and the Regions – Tenth Report*, UK Office of the Deputy Prime Minister, London.

UK ODPM (2004a), *Housing in England 2002/3: A Report Principally from the 2002/2003 Survey of English Housing*, UK Office of the Deputy Prime Minister, London.

UK ODPM (2004b), *Housing Act 2004: Fact Sheets*, UK Office of the Deputy Prime Minister, London.

UK ODPM (2004c), *Housing Act 2004: Regulatory Impact Assessments*, UK Office of the Deputy Prime Minister, London.

UK ODPM (2005), *Lessons from the Past, Challenges for Future for Housing Policy*, UK Office of the Deputy Prime Minister, London.

Urban White Paper (2000), "Our Towns and Cities: The Future – Delivering Urban Renaissance", Office of the Deputy Prime Minister, United Kingdom *www.odpm.gov.uk/index.asp?id=1127168*.

Vicario, L. and P. M. Martínez Monje (2003), "Another 'Guggenheim Effect'? The Generation of a Potentially Gentrifiable Neighbourhood in Bilbao", *Urban Studies*, Vol. 40, No. 12, pp. 2383-2400.

Ward, S.V. (2002), *Planning the Twentieth-Century City – The Advanced Capitalist World*, John Wiley and Sons, New Jersey.

Whitehead, C. M. E. (1991), "From Need to Affordability: An Analysis of UK Housing Objectives", *Urban Studies*, Vol. 28, No. 6, pp. 871-887.

OECD PUBLICATIONS, 2, rue André-Pascal, 75775 PARIS CEDEX 16
PRINTED IN FRANCE
(04 2007 05 1 P) ISBN 978-92-64-02240-9 – No. 55551 2007

CPSIA information can be obtained
at www.ICGtesting.com
Printed in the USA
JSHW022130130920
7837JS00001B/7